FOR THE LOVE OF THE
AIR FORCE

A COMPANION

NORMAN FERGUSON

summersdale

FOR THE LOVE OF THE AIR FORCE

An Hachette UK Company
www.hachette.co.uk

Summersdale Publishers Ltd
Part of Octopus Publishing Group Limited
Carmelite House
50 Victoria Embankment
LONDON
EC4Y 0DZ
UK

www.summersdale.com

Printed and bound in China

ISBN: 978-1-78685-065-2

Substantial discounts on bulk quantities of Summersdale books are available to corporations, professional associations and other organisations. For details contact general enquiries: telephone: +44 (0) 1243 771107 or email: enquiries@summersdale.com.

Per ardua ad astra
(Through adversity to the stars)

MOTTO OF THE RAF

This book is dedicated to all the men and women who have served in the RAF in its first 100 years.

CONTENTS

FOREWORD..7
INTRODUCTION..9

PART 1: HISTORY...11
Chapter 1: Beginnings...13
Chapter 2: Between the Wars......................................23
Chapter 3: Second World War.....................................35
Chapter 4: Beyond the Second World War....................57

PART 2: THE ARMS..89
Chapter 5: Trades and Branches..................................91
Chapter 6: Squadrons..106
Chapter 7: Reserves and Auxiliaries............................127
Chapter 8: Women in the Service...............................133
Chapter 9: Training..140
Chapter 10: Air Cadets...153
Chapter 11: Public Face of the RAF............................157

PART 3: THE SERVICE..165
Chapter 12: Ranks, Badges, Uniforms and Medals.........167
Chapter 13: Life in the Service..................................191

PART 4: THE TECHNOLOGY....................................207
Chapter 14: The Aircraft...209
Chapter 15: Engines, Weapons and Equipment......................222

PART 5: MEMORIALS..257
Chapter 16: Memorials..259

THE FUTURE..265
SOURCES..267
ACKNOWLEDGEMENTS..271

FOREWORD

In April 2018, the Royal Air Force celebrates the 100th anniversary of its formation, so it is very appropriate that *For the Love of the Air Force* is published at this time. For the Service, the period since 1918 has been very eventful as military aviation advanced from simple aircraft with a simple role to the very complicated and extremely capable machines of today. There have been two world wars, a lengthy Cold War and dozens of minor conflicts; almost continually from its formation, the Royal Air Force has been distinguishing itself in action somewhere in the world for approaching 100 years.

To compress all of that into just 270 pages was a tall order but Norman Ferguson has been very successful indeed. The history, the people, the aircraft, the weapons, the operations and the units are all included, as are the ranks, the badges, the uniforms, the medals, the Air Cadets and the memorials. The author also includes a few of the things that didn't go quite right. This combination makes the book a most useful compendium of information about the Service which is written in a readable style and I believe it will feature on the bookshelves of many aviation enthusiasts. It will also be an ideal present for any young person who has an interest in such things.

Air Marshal Sir Roger Austin KCB AFC, June 2017

INTRODUCTION

Although in existence for only a century, Britain's air force is one of its most recognisable public institutions. Its history contains the exploits of Edward Mannock, Douglas Bader, Guy Gibson and Leonard Cheshire; its aircraft include the Sopwith Camel, the Spitfire, the Lancaster, the Mosquito, the Lightning, the Vulcan and the Harrier; its bases include Biggin Hill, Tangmere, Scampton, Duxford and Hendon.

This book will tell the story of this first century of the 'junior service' through chapters on its history, its people and all its associated elements. It will also tell of life in the blue uniform and some of the traditions of the service, as well as looking at the current organisation.

My own first-hand experiences of the RAF are from the outside, as a member of the Air Training Corps visiting some of the bases that were part of the front line of the Cold War, as both a cadet and an aviation enthusiast. The personnel's quiet humour, allied to a strong sense of professionalism, is a constant thread running through their history. Those who wore the blue uniform had a serious job to do but did not always take themselves too seriously. I hope they find plenty to inform and entertain within these pages.

Norman Ferguson, 2017

PART 1

HISTORY

CHAPTER ONE

BEGINNINGS

Military aviation began in the UK with balloon flying. Trials to ascertain their potential were started in the 1860s while a unit of the Royal Engineers operated static balloons for observation purposes from the 1890s. They were deployed with some success in the Boer War although army commanders were not convinced of their usefulness, with some worried that they would frighten the horses.

Following the Wright brothers' flight of 1903, it was a fellow American who made the first fixed-wing, powered aircraft flight in the UK. On 16 October 1908, former Wild West showman Samuel Franklin Cody took to the skies at what would become a famous aeronautical site, Farnborough in Hampshire.

Cody advocated the use of aircraft for military purposes, but it took several years for the opportunities of fixed-wing military aviation to be realised. In 1912, trials were held to choose an aircraft for the newly formed Royal Flying Corps (RFC) and although Cody's 'flying cathedral' design won, the production order was given to the Royal Aircraft Factory's BE.2 instead.

The BE.2 was to serve for several years in the RFC, which was formed in April 1912 with a Military Wing and a Naval Wing. The navy was not amenable to losing control over its air arm and so went its own way, establishing its Royal Naval Air Service (RNAS) in 1914. The First Lord of the Admiralty at the time was a certain Winston Churchill, who had trained as a pilot and was aware of the potential benefits of military aviation in any future conflict.

FIRST WORLD WAR

'Aviation is fine as a sport but as an instrument of war, it is worthless.'
FRENCH COMMANDER GENERAL FERDINAND FOCH IN 1911

When war broke out in August 1914 the RFC sent most of its viable aircraft across the English Channel. Four squadrons and a reserve called the Aircraft Park arrived in France – the first-ever overseas deployment of British military aircraft. The 63 machines were a mixture of BE.2a, BE.8, Avro 504 and Henri Farman F.20 biplanes, along with Blériot XI monoplanes.

Before they left for the Continent pilots were issued with orders as to which items were to be carried:

- ▶ revolver
- ▶ field glasses
- ▶ spare goggles
- ▶ a roll of tools
- ▶ water bottle (containing boiled water)
- ▶ stove
- ▶ haversack
- ▶ biscuits
- ▶ cold meat
- ▶ a piece of chocolate
- ▶ dried soup mix.

At the front

The ground crews and equipment were transported by ship and, once established, RFC pilots were tasked with reconnaissance missions. They played an important part in the British Expeditionary Force's (BEF) awareness of the German army's advance and prevented it being outflanked at the Battle of Mons. This work was recognised by commander-in-chief of the BEF, General Sir John French, in a dispatch of 7 September:

> *'They have furnished me with the most complete and accurate information which has been of incalculable value in the conduct of operations. Fired at constantly both by friend and foe, and not hesitating to fly in every kind of weather, they have remained undaunted throughout.'*

Royal Naval Air Service

Britain's other military air force was also operating on the Continent. The RNAS had flown its own mixture of types over to Ostend at the end of August. They carried out the first long-range bombing missions when its machines attacked Zeppelin sheds at Düsseldorf and Cologne in September and October. The raid on 8 October saw spectacular results when the Zeppelin inside its hangar was hit by bombs dropped by a Sopwith Tabloid. Navy flyers followed this with an audacious, 250-mile round trip to bomb the Zeppelin works at Friedrichshafen on Lake Constance. Three Avro 504s flew at low level with one being brought down by enemy ground fire.

New roles

When the front line became static on the Western Front the RFC found new roles: artillery spotting and photo reconnaissance. These required steady flying over enemy territory, which made the crews vulnerable to fire from German aircraft and anti-aircraft artillery. Another task carried out was that of contact patrols, to spot the position of British troops during an attack – but it was not wholly successful, with troops unwilling to reveal their position.

The RFC's aircraft were initially unarmed, but pilots and observers took their own weapons aloft and in August 1914 a rifle was used to bring down a German Taube monoplane. Machine guns were added and aircraft were subsequently designed specifically for aerial combat – with one example being the world's first pure fighter, the Vickers FB.5 'Gunbus', which was armed with a single Lewis machine gun.

The threat increased in July 1915 when the German Fokker Eindecker monoplane arrived. It had a single forward-firing machine gun that was synchronised to fire through the propeller, thus giving the pilot increased accuracy and control. German aces Oswald Boelcke and Max Immelmann flew Eindeckers in what was known as the 'Fokker Scourge' – when Germany dominated the skies.

New tactics were brought in as the war progressed. Support for ground troops was increased as Allied generals adapted and developed new tactics. When tanks were introduced, aircraft flew low overhead to mask the engine noise to preserve the element of surprise. By 1918, Sopwith Camels were flying low level to strafe German positions.

DID YOU KNOW?

The famous RAF roundel was inspired by one used by the French. British aircraft were coming under fire from their own side and so it was decided it would be best to emblazon each aircraft with identifying markings. The Union Jack was initially painted on aircraft, but from a distance its similarity to the German Iron Cross made its use unsustainable. The French-style roundel was then applied, albeit with a reversal of the colours, so that blue was on the outside and red in the centre, with a white band in between.

In 1915 British manufacturers began to produce what we recognise as a fighter: single-crewed, single-engined, manoeuvrable and properly armed – an aircraft specifically designed to bring down other aircraft. The Airco DH.2 had a fixed machine gun and effectively countered the 'Fokker Scourge', entering service in February 1916. In a technological battle, more types soon arrived, such as the Sopwith Pup in late 1916 and the Sopwith Camel in 1917.

GREAT AIRCRAFT: SOPWITH CAMEL

Maximum speed: 117 mph
Maximum altitude: 19,000 ft
Armament: 2 x Vickers machine guns
Crew: 1

This 'fierce little beast', as described by one pilot, was a highly effective fighter: Camels shot down 1,294 aircraft, the most by any Allied fighter. However, its great strength and its greatest weakness were the two sides of a coin: manoeuvrability also meant instability; it could turn quickly, but a less than capable pilot could easily end up in trouble. Almost 800 pilots died flying Camels, predominantly in training accidents.

> 'As I looked at the machine I saw the enemy gunner
> fall away from the Hannover fuselage. I had no
> feeling for him for I knew he was dead, for I had
> fired three hundred rounds of ammunition at very
> close range and I must have got 90 per cent hits.'

JAMES MCCUDDEN IN FLYING FURY: FIVE YEARS IN THE ROYAL FLYING CORPS (1918)

GREAT AIRCRAFT: BRISTOL F.2B FIGHTER

Maximum speed: 125 mph
Maximum altitude: 20,000 ft
Armament: 1 x Vickers machine gun and 1 or 2 x Lewis machine guns
Crew: 2

The 'Brisfit' was a two-seater, with an observer operating a rearward-firing machine gun. When first introduced in April 1917, the F.2a version was flown sedately and suffered losses, but when it was discovered to be strong and able to turn as well as a single-seater it was flown to its capabilities and became a valuable fighter. The F.2b version came with a more powerful engine and in the Middle East campaign it took part in the rout of Turkish forces in Sinai. It was in service until the 1930s, with 5,308 being made in total.

Bombing

In the early stages of the war, bombs or grenades were dropped but they were small in size and not subject to much in the way of guidance aids, with some being hand-dropped over the side of the fuselage.

Improvements in aiming came in the form of bombsights, and by 1916 squadrons were carrying out massed raids on enemy targets such as airfields and ammunition dumps. While carrying a bombload, aircraft were not able to manoeuvre well against enemy fighters, so the bombing took place at night. This improved survivability but reduced accuracy.

DID YOU KNOW?

In August 1918 an Airco DH.4 of 205 Sqn brought down a German Pfalz by deliberately dropping a bomb on to it.

GREAT AIRCRAFT: AIRCO DH.9A

Maximum speed: 123 mph*
Maximum altitude: 16,500 ft*
Armament: 1 x Vickers forward-firing (fixed) machine gun,
                                    1 or 2 x Lewis rearward-firing machine guns;
                                    660 lb bombload
Crew: 2

The DH.9 had succeeded the effective and well-regarded DH.4 as a day bomber, but the first version was underpowered. The DH.9A, which entered service in June 1918, had a more powerful engine, either the 375 hp Rolls-Royce Eagle or the 400 hp Liberty V-type. Almost 900 were produced during wartime. DH.9As continued to be flown until the early 1930s, being used overseas in the 'air control' era.

*Version with Liberty engine.

Air defence

Aircraft began to be used in 1915 for UK air defence against Zeppelin and Schütte-Lanz airships, then later against Gotha bombers. These raids tested the British civilian population's resolve; one raid on London in June 1916 killed 162 people.

The military came under pressure to counter these attacks and the defence force grew to 12 RFC squadrons with 12,000 men employed in anti-aircraft artillery batteries. Even with the size of the airships and their relatively slow speed it was hard to find them, and at night it was doubly difficult. With searchlights and anti-aircraft guns the defences were improved, and new technology in the shape of improved incendiary and explosive bullets for the fighters' machine guns saw success when the first Zeppelin was brought down over the UK in September 1916. By the war's end German air raids had caused the deaths of 1,414 civilians, with another 4,000 wounded.

DID YOU KNOW?

The first air supply drop was made in 1916 during the siege of Kut-al-Amara in Iraq. A besieged British army force received 19,000 lb of supplies including salt, sugar and other food, as well as opium, medical supplies, money, radio spare parts and a 70-pound millstone, which were dropped by parachute. Attempts to relieve the siege failed and the soldiers were forced to surrender.

A new service

During the war it was clear there was great inter-service rivalry and inefficiencies in supply of aircraft. South African General Jan Smuts was asked to look at these problems and in August 1917 he proposed the establishment of a Royal Air Force and an overseeing Air Ministry and Air Staff. This new organisation, amalgamating the RFC and RNAS, came into being on 1 April 1918 and took over all military aviation functions. It was the world's first independent air force. At the time the RFC had 118 squadrons and the RNAS had 50. Seventy-six were in France and 24 in other areas overseas with the rest based in the UK.

GREAT MEN OF THE AIR FORCE
EDWARD MANNOCK

Mannock differed from most of his fellow pilots in that he came from a working-class background and was a socialist. Despite initial misgivings amongst some of his colleagues, Mannock proved himself in the air and became commanding officer of 84 Sqn. He emphasised the value of training and teamwork amongst his pilots, whom he inspired to become effective combat aviators.

Mannock was well aware of the dangers of flying and fighting in the air and he carried a revolver in order not to suffer the excruciating pain of a 'flamerino' – the spiralling descent of an aircraft on fire. When famed German ace Manfred von Richthofen was killed, Mannock said, 'I hope the bastard roasted all the way down.'

Mannock died in July 1918 while showing a new pilot the ropes. He had attained 61 certified kills and in 1919 was posthumously awarded the Victoria Cross.

GREAT AIRCRAFT: ROYAL AIRCRAFT FACTORY SE.5A

Maximum speed:	138 mph
Maximum altitude:	20,000 ft
Armament:	1 x Vickers machine gun and 1 x Lewis machine gun
Crew:	1

The SE.5a is regarded as the best British fighter of the war. It was fast, manoeuvrable and stable, which meant inexperienced pilots could have confidence in its handling. The SE.5a helped establish Allied air superiority in 1917 and was flown by aces such as Albert Ball, Edward Mannock and James McCudden.

Independent Air Force

In June 1918 the Independent Air Force was formed to launch long-range bombing missions against strategic targets in Germany. Airco DH.4s and DH.9s were used for day bombing, and night operations were carried out by Royal Aircraft Factory FE.2s and Handley Page O/400s.

Despite heavy losses in the day-bombing units, which lost 256 men in five months of operation, and although it had not proven hugely effective, the idea of a strategic bombing force was one that would return to the thinking of military commanders and politicians in the not-too-distant future.

'What I want is a bloody paralyser not a toy.'
COMMODORE MURRAY SUETER, DIRECTOR OF THE
ADMIRALTY'S AIR DEPARTMENT. SUETER WISHED TO IMPRESS
ON AIRCRAFT DESIGNER AND COMPANY OWNER FREDERICK
HANDLEY PAGE HIS DESIRE FOR A HEAVY BOMBER. THE
BOMBER BECAME THE HANDLEY PAGE O/400, ABLE TO CARRY
A 2,000 LB BOMBLOAD.

'A LITTLE HELL(P) FROM THE RAF'
INSCRIPTION PAINTED ON A 1,650 LB BOMB – THE RAF'S
BIGGEST OF THE WAR – DROPPED BY AN O/400 IN AUGUST
1918 ON LE CATEAU RAILWAY STATION

DID YOU KNOW?

British aircraft fought in Russia. Aircraft and men were
deployed in support of anti-Bolshevik forces following
the Revolution of 1917. They continued to be involved
until 1920.

CHAPTER TWO
BETWEEN THE WARS

The First World War ended with the RAF the biggest air force in the world, comprising 22,000 aircraft and almost 300,000 personnel; however, its pre-eminent place was not to last. By the end of 1919 it had lost 176 of its operational wartime squadrons, leaving just 12. In terms of personnel it was reduced to little more than a tenth of its previous size, with just 31,500 officers and men.

The new 'junior service' was under pressure for its very existence from the army and navy, both of which were concerned their tactical requirements would not be met. In 1919 Chief of the Air Staff Sir Hugh Trenchard prepared a white paper entitled 'An Outline of the Scheme for the Permanent Organisation of the Royal Air Force'. The paper, also known as 'The Trenchard Memorandum', assumed there was no imminent need for general mobilisation but that the RAF should be organised so that it could expand efficiently in future years if required. Training was fundamental for officers and men. A small reserve would be retained in the UK and sufficient squadrons would be provided for overseas garrisons. In the financially straitened post-war period Trenchard argued that air power was less expensive to use overseas than land forces. A passage in the paper outlined a future role for the RAF:

'Recent events have shown the value of aircraft in dealing with frontier troubles and it is not perhaps too much to hope that before long it may prove possible to regard the Royal Air Force units not as an addition to the military garrison but as a substitute for part of it.'

Despite this, the pressure continued with the navy particularly keen on establishing control over their own air assets. The arrangement in place at the time was that the navy operated the aircraft carriers but the air force owned the aircraft. The First Sea Lord, Earl Beatty, threatened to resign if more control was not granted, but Lord Salisbury investigated the issue, which resulted in the air force being given a vote of confidence in plans being laid for its expansion. By the end of 1924 the RAF had 43 squadrons, but it was not expanded to the size envisaged by the Salisbury Committee due to factors such as the state of the economy and the feeling that peace would endure.

'We intend to pursue the organisation of imperial defence on the existing basis of three co-equal services. It is in the interests of the fighting services that controversy upon this subject should now cease.'
PRIME MINISTER STANLEY BALDWIN, HOUSE OF COMMONS, 25 FEBRUARY 1926

However, it did not cease and in 1937 the navy's aircraft as part of its Fleet Air Arm returned to Admiralty control.

AIR CONTROL
Trenchard's promotion of the RAF in the aerial policing role was put to the test in the years after the First World War in different parts of the Empire. This 'control without occupation' policy used First World War aircraft such as the Bristol Fighter and DH.9A. They remained in service until they were replaced in the early 1930s

by the Westland Wapiti, which in order to save money utilised as many components of the DH.9A as possible. Soldiers were transported in troop carriers such as the Vickers Victoria. Aircraft in aerial policing roles would drop leaflets on tribal villages warning the local population (who couldn't always read) of the imminent bombing raids.

Afghanistan

In 1919 two squadrons had flown in support of the army in the Third Afghan War. One of the missions saw a Handley Page V/1500 bomb the palace of Amir Amanullah Khan in Kabul. The air force's actions contributed to the end of the short, four-week war, but further bombing was carried out against Afghan tribes. The RAF was not able to operate freely as the tribesmen were able to shoot down several aircraft through accurate rifle fire. Eventually, by the spring of 1920, the air campaign saw results. In 1928 the air force was called into action when trouble flared up against the Amir. The British embassy was surrounded and from December 1928 to February 1929 transporters flew out the recently abdicated Amir Amanullah and almost 600 of the embassy's staff, along with other foreign nationals, in one of the world's first airlift operations.

British Somaliland

One of the most successful uses of aircraft overseas was in British Somaliland against tribal leader Mohammed Abdullah Hassan, given the nickname the 'Mad Mullah'. In January 1920 12 DH.9s of 'Z' Force operated in conjunction with ground forces such as the Somaliland Camel Corps until the rebellious Hassan was forced to flee to Abyssinia.

Iraq

Following this success in Somaliland, another area that saw the use of aerial resources was Mesopotamia (now Iraq). In 1920 an uprising of 130,000 tribesmen had been suppressed by the British Army, which saw around 400 soldiers killed. Apart from the human cost, the government was keen to make savings in its overseas budget and Winston Churchill, who was now Colonial Secretary, asked Trenchard if the air force would be able to take this on, as stretched budgets would not allow expenditure on sufficient ground forces and would thus give the service an opportunity to show what it could do. Trenchard, who was keen to demonstrate the usefulness of his air force, accepted.

Ground forces were still required and local irregular forces (Iraq Levies) were recruited alongside air force armoured car units and nine battalions of Indian and British troops. These, along with eight squadrons of aircraft, were put under the command of Air Vice-Marshal John Salmond in October 1922.

Trouble arose in the north of Iraq when Kurds under Sheikh Mahmud Barzanji – the self-styled 'King of Kurdistan' – began an uprising. This was initially suppressed by aircraft and ground troops. The aircraft not only dropped bombs but carried troops and supplies in the world's first aerial troop lift; they also acted to evacuate the wounded. Mahmud fled but returned and actions against him continued until 1931.

The RAF, operating from four bases – Hinaidi, Mosul, Baghdad and Shaibah – had shown how effective air power could be and kept overall responsibility for Iraq until 1932. The financial benefits to the Treasury were also considerable: in 1921–22 the British spent £23.3 million governing Iraq; by 1927 the amount was £3.9 million.

Turkey
In 1922 a confrontation in western Turkey with Turkish forces under Kemal Atatürk, the former commander at Gallipoli, saw a large force of land-based aircraft and those on aircraft carriers called in. Although no combat took place, the air force showed it was able to respond appropriately to such a crisis.

Palestine and Aden
The success in aerial policing saw the air force given responsibility for Palestine and Aden. Aircraft were initially utilised against raiding

tribesmen from Syria as well as within Palestine itself. Their ability to intervene in the trouble between Jews and Arabs was limited due to the urban nature and closeness in location of the two sides' territories but involvement in Palestine continued into the 1930s and aircraft such as Hawker Harts and Hinds were used to enforce 'air cordoning' – the imposition of blockading from the air. In Aden in 1928, armoured cars and DH.9As, then later on Fairey IIIfs, were used against local tribesmen.

India

Aircraft were sent out to India in 1915. BE.2cs of 32 Sqn were shipped to Bombay then on to the North-West Frontier between India and Afghanistan (now part of Pakistan) where they were engaged against tribes in the Khyber Pass.

By 1924 six squadrons were in action against Mahsud tribesmen in Waziristan, most of whom accepted peace terms. In 1925 'Pink's War' – named for Wing Commander Richard Pink who was in charge of aerial forces in the area – saw aircraft used without ground troops. After eight weeks of bombing, the tribesmen agreed terms. Other bombing missions were carried out against dissident tribes in the following years although it was otherwise a period of relative peace.

In 1930 rebellions in Peshawar and Waziristan were countered by intensive air operations that included daily bombing missions that ran for six weeks.

Summary

The role of the RAF in maintaining British control of its Empire is one that no doubt helped protect the new service's very existence. The amount of civilian casualties that resulted – collateral damage in modern parlance – was not something which at the time prevented the policy being deemed a great success.

DID YOU KNOW?

During the 1920s the air force used psychological warfare. Vickers Valentias and Victorias carried loudspeakers on the underside of their fuselages, through which broadcasts, or 'sky shouting', were made to local populations in Iraq, India and Somaliland.

GREAT MEN OF THE AIR FORCE
HUGH TRENCHARD

'For nearly twenty years I watched the army and the navy, both singly and in concert, engineer one deliberate attempt after another to destroy the Royal Air Force. Time after time they were within a hairbreadth of success: time after time Trenchard, and Trenchard alone, saved us.'

SIR ARTHUR HARRIS, COMMANDER-IN-CHIEF, BOMBER COMMAND, WRITING IN 1947

Known as 'Boom' for his powerful voice, Hugh Trenchard had served in the Boer War as a cavalry officer and in 1912, looking for a new challenge, had learnt to fly. He became Assistant Commandant of the Central Flying School and then Commander of the RFC's Military Wing at Farnborough where his organisational skills were put to great use.

He became head of the RFC in France in August 1915, visited all the corps' bases and listened to the men under his command. He saw the potential for the use of aircraft in warfare and advocated a policy of sustained aerial aggression in order to control the skies above the battlefield and allow the bombing of industrial targets that supplied the enemy's front line. Trenchard's policy meant RFC aircrew were always operating over German-held territory, which put them at a disadvantage in being recovered if they made forced landings. His aggressive policy also meant he was against pilots and observers being given parachutes (in case they abandoned functioning machines too early due to a lack of fighting spirit), which led to unnecessary loss of life. British balloon crews were given parachutes, as were German pilots and observers.

In January 1918 Trenchard was appointed Chief of the Air Staff but was unable to work with the Air Minister, Lord Rothermere, and resigned soon afterwards. In June 1918 he took command of the new Independent Force, which he described as 'a gigantic waste of effort and personnel', believing its resources could have been better put to the aid of the British Expeditionary Force. However, he did see the advantage of such bombing and believed it could defeat Germany's resolve through the disintegration of morale amongst the civilian population in a future conflict.

In 1919 Winston Churchill, who was now Air Minister, appointed Trenchard as Chief of the Air Staff for the second time. During his 10 years in the post, Trenchard oversaw the reduction in size of the post-war RAF but earned the name 'father of the Royal Air Force' for the new initiatives he brought in. These included:

- ▶ an officer training college at Cranwell
- ▶ an apprentice school at Halton
- ▶ a staff college at Andover
- ▶ the Auxiliary Air Force
- ▶ short service commissions
- ▶ a benevolent fund for ex-personnel.

Trenchard also defended the RAF's independence from moves by the army and navy to split it up. The 'control without occupation' strategy of policing British colonial territories from the air showed the organisation's effectiveness. He was made the first Marshal of the RAF in 1927. After leaving the service, he was Commissioner of the Metropolitan Police and served on the board of the United Africa Company. Trenchard died in 1956 and was buried at Westminster Abbey.

AIRCRAFT PROCUREMENT

After the war aircraft procurement was slowed down and types were kept in service for longer than might have been expected. The Bristol Fighter was only retired in the 1930s.

Biplanes remained as the basic aircraft design in the decades after the First World War. Aircraft such as the Fairey Fox and the Hawker Fury were fine examples of the biplane but the limitations of the twin-wing layout were reached with the four-gun Gloster Gladiator – the last British biplane fighter to be flown in front-line service.

Heavier bomber types such as the Vickers Virginia and the Handley Page Heyford were in service during the 1930s, although neither posed any serious threat to Nazi Germany, being limited in both range and bombload.

GREAT AIRCRAFT: HAWKER FURY

Maximum speed: 223 mph
Maximum altitude: 29,500 ft
Armament: 2 x Vickers machine guns
Crew: 1

Entering service with 43 Sqn in 1931 the elegant Fury was the first air force aircraft to fly faster than 200 mph in level flight. Its powerful 525 hp Kestrel engine made it ideal for aerobatics and Furies were noted for their appearances at Hendon displays. The type was replaced by the Gladiator and the Hurricane in the late 1930s.

DID YOU KNOW?

The RAF pioneered many of the routes that were later used by the Imperial Airways civilian airline. Routes such as Cairo to Baghdad, Cairo to South Africa and the UK to Singapore were flown in the 1920s.

RECORD FLIGHTS

Air force crews set several world records in the 1930s:

- ▶ In September 1931 Flight Lieutenant George Stainforth became the first pilot to fly faster than 400 mph in setting a new speed record of 407.5 mph. The feat was achieved in the Supermarine S.6B that had recently won the Schneider Trophy seaplane competition outright for the UK.

- ▶ Squadron Leader Gayford and Flight Lieutenant Nicholetts flew 5,410 miles from Cranwell to Walvis Bay in south-west Africa non-stop in February 1933 in a Fairey Long-range Monoplane. The specially designed type had been used to fly the first non-stop flight from the UK to India in 1929 – a journey that took 50 hours 37 minutes.

- ▶ The most famous of the record-breaking flights was on 3 April 1933 when Flight Lieutenant David McIntyre and Squadron Leader Douglas Douglas-Hamilton of the Auxiliary Air Force were the first to fly over Mount Everest, in a Westland Wallace and a Houston-Westland respectively.

- ▶ In September 1936, wearing a special pressure suit, Squadron Leader F. R. D. Swain set an altitude record when he flew a Bristol 138 monoplane to a height of 49,967 ft. The record was later pushed higher still, with 53,937 ft being reached by Flight Lieutenant Maurice Adam in June 1937.

WHEN THINGS DON'T GO RIGHT: HEYFORDS

In December 1936 seven Handley Page Heyford bombers of 102 Sqn were returning to Finningley from Aldergrove in Northern Ireland when they flew into thick fog and freezing conditions. Three of the bombers crashed and three force-landed. Only one arrived intact. Three crewmen were killed and another three were injured.

EXPANSION

The Ruhr crisis of 1923 arose when France and Belgium occupied the Ruhr valley when Germany failed to keep paying its First World War reparations. It raised the prospect of war with a continental nation, so the Home Defence Air Force was established to protect the UK. It was felt the air force should have parity with the biggest of potential enemy air forces, and with this in mind it was decided that 52 squadrons would be needed. Trenchard believed that most of these squadrons should be equipped with bombers, to form a strategic deterrence, with the split being 17 fighter and 35 bomber squadrons. However, the planned expansion scheme was slowed down and the 52 squadrons would not be fully in place until the middle of the next decade.

In 1925 the Air Defence of Great Britain command was established under Air Vice-Marshal Sir John Salmond, made up of fighter aircraft squadrons, army anti-aircraft guns, searchlights and the Observer Corps.

THREAT FROM GERMANY

The 1930s saw the rise of Nazism in Germany, with Hitler covertly rearming and testing the Allied powers through territorial expansion despite this contravening the provisions of the 1919 Treaty of Versailles. The UK government, which had slowed down its expansion plans of the mid-1920s, witnessed the failure of the Geneva Disarmament Conference during the 1930s and had no option but to rearm in order to deter German aggression.

Between 1934 and 1938 the Air Ministry oversaw a series of schemes for expansion. They specified the number of aircraft and squadrons to be brought into service in plans approved by the cabinet, though in the event only one such initiative was completed. But in 1937 Sir Thomas Inskip, Minister for Co-ordination of Defence, had been asked to carry out a review of air defence and his report changed priorities from bombers to fighters – a shift that would be of crucial importance.

Because of the foresight of those charged with aircraft procurement the RAF received aircraft in the form of the Hawker Hurricane and Vickers-Supermarine Spitfire that were technologically advanced: monoplanes with retractable undercarriage, eight machine guns and more powerful engines, allowing greater speeds and higher altitudes.

WHEN THINGS DON'T GO RIGHT: K7036

On 10 March 1937 the very first Bristol Blenheim due to be delivered to a squadron was landing at Wyton when the pilot over-braked. The monoplane flipped over on to its back and was damaged beyond repair.

BOMBING

'The bomber will always get through. The only defence is in offence, which means that you have to kill more women and children more quickly than the enemy if you want to save yourselves.'
PRIME MINISTER STANLEY BALDWIN, 1932

In the 1930s the idea of effecting military victory through strategic bombing gained much attention. Trenchard thought that to be on the offensive was vital and that bombing could destroy a country's military production capability, its communication network and the morale of its people. Bombing alone would not win a war, but in conjunction with ground forces it would play a hugely important part.

Novels and movies of the time, such as H. G. Wells's *Things to Come*, depicted the terror that would result from an aerial assault. Real-life events such as the Japanese bombing of Shanghai in 1932 and the German attacks in the Spanish Civil War, particularly at Guernica in 1937, compounded memories of First World War air raids. A government committee of 1937 estimated that German bombers would kill 58,000 civilians each day in any coming conflict.

CHAPTER THREE

SECOND WORLD WAR

TIMELINE

SEPTEMBER 1939

3   Britain declares war on Germany.

A Bristol Blenheim of 13 Sqn is the first UK aircraft to fly over Germany in the war.

4   Sergeant George Booth becomes the first British prisoner of war when his Blenheim is shot down over Germany.

6   The Battle of Barking Creek sees the first UK fighter pilot fatality of the war.

20   A German Messerschmitt Me 109 becomes the first aircraft shot down by the air force in the war, by an 88 Sqn Fairey Battle.

OCTOBER 1939

16 602 (City of Glasgow) and 603 (City of Edinburgh) Auxiliary Air Force Sqns shoot down the first German aircraft over the UK.

DECEMBER 1939

18 Half the Wellington bombers in a raid on Wilhelmshaven are lost; day bombing is suspended.

MAY 1940

12 Flying Officer D. E. Garland and Sergeant T. Gray of 12 Sqn are killed attacking a bridge in Belgium. They become the first air force personnel to be awarded the Victoria Cross in the war.

JUNE 1940

4 RAF aircraft cover the last day of the Dunkirk evacuation.

18 The last Hurricanes leave France.

JULY 1940

10 The Battle of Britain begins.

AUGUST 1940

2 The first Hurricanes are delivered to defend Malta.

18 The 'Hardest Day' of the Battle of Britain sees the heaviest total losses, with the RAF and Luftwaffe losing 100 aircraft between them.

SEPTEMBER 1940

7 The Luftwaffe turns its attention away from military airfields and bombs London.

15 The Luftwaffe launches a large raid on London, which is successfully met by Fighter Command.

OCTOBER 1940

31   The Battle of Britain ends.

NOVEMBER 1940

19   Flight Lieutenant John Cunningham is the first Bristol Beaufighter night fighter pilot to shoot down a German bomber. He goes on to become one of the RAF's most successful pilots in this role.

MAY 1941

26   The German battleship *Bismarck* is spotted by a Coastal Command Catalina. The ship is sunk by Fleet Air Arm Fairey Swordfishes and navy ships.

JUNE 1941

14   Aircraft support British troops in Operation Battleaxe to relieve the siege of Tobruk. The operation is not successful.

AUGUST 1941

9   Douglas Bader is shot down over France. As one of his prosthetic legs was lost in the crash, another is parachuted down to him.

OCTOBER 1941

9   The Western Desert Air Force is formed to carry out air operations in North Africa.

DECEMBER 1941

8   Following Japan's entry into the war, British and Royal Australian Air Force (RAAF) aircraft attack Japanese targets in Malaya.

FEBRUARY 1942

1   The RAF Regiment is formed to defend air force establishments.

11/12   The 'Channel Dash' sees German warships slip through the English Channel despite the aircraft and ships tasked with their engagement.

22   Air Marshal Arthur Harris becomes Commander-in-Chief of Bomber Command.

MARCH 1942
7   The first Spitfires arrive on Malta during the island's heavy bombardment.

MAY 1942
30/31   The first of Bomber Command's 1,000-bomber raids – on Cologne.

JUNE 1942
12   A 236 Sqn Beaufighter flies over Paris at low level and drops a Tricolour over the Arc de Triomphe. The crew of Flight Lieutenant A. K. Gatward and Sergeant G. Fern then strafe a Gestapo HQ.

AUGUST 1942
15   Bomber Command's precision marking unit, the Pathfinder Force, is formed.

19   RAF aircraft fly in support of troops landed at Dieppe.

SEPTEMBER 1942
19   Mosquitoes carry out the first daylight raid on Berlin.

MAY 1943
16/17   617 Sqn attack the Ruhr dams.

JULY 1943
9/10   Aircraft tow gliders, drop parachutists and provide cover for the Sicily landings.

24/25   Operation Gomorrah – the bombing of Hamburg – begins.

AUGUST 1943
17/18   Bomber Command attacks V2 rocket production facilities at Peenemünde.

SEPTEMBER 1943
15/16   617 Sqn attacks the Dortmund–Ems Canal with 12,000 lb bombs.

NOVEMBER 1943
18/19   The Battle of Berlin begins.

FEBRUARY 1944
18   Mosquitoes attack Amiens prison in a low-level raid to free French Resistance prisoners. Their precision strike allows over 250 to escape, although 102 are killed in the bombing.

MARCH 1944
5/6   British and American aircraft transport Orde Wingate's Chindits to positions hundreds of miles behind Japanese lines.

16   At Imphal in India, British troops are cut off by Japanese forces and have to be resupplied by air. The same happens at Kohima the following month.

24/25   'The Great Escape' takes place as 76 prisoners of war, led by Squadron Leader Roger Bushell, escape through a tunnel at Stalag Luft III. Fifty of the 73 recaptured escapees are shot on Hitler's orders.

30/31   Bomber Command suffers its biggest losses in one attack, with 95 aircraft failing to return from Nuremberg.

JUNE 1944

6   The D-Day landings in Normandy are supported by RAF aircraft in various roles that include bombing, reconnaissance, fleet defence, decoy runs, paratrooper transportation, glider towing and tactical support.

8/9   The Saumur rail tunnel is blocked by 617 Sqn dropping 12,000 lb 'Tallboy' penetration bombs.

13   V1 flying bombs are launched for the first time against London. RAF aircraft develop techniques to intercept this new type of weapon.

JULY 1944

12   The Gloster Meteor enters service – the UK's first operational jet aircraft.

AUGUST 1944

7   Hawker Typhoons play a major part in stopping a German counter-attack at Falaise in Normandy.

SEPTEMBER 1944

17   Allied transport aircraft carry parachutists and tow gliders towards Arnhem as part of Operation Market Garden.

NOVEMBER 1944

12   The *Tirpitz* capsizes after bombing by 9 and 617 Sqns near Tromsø in Norway.

FEBRUARY 1945

13/14   The German city of Dresden is bombed; 25,000 are killed.

MARCH 1945

14   617 Sqn successfully drop 22,000 lb 'Grand Slam' bombs on Bielefeld railway viaduct.

24   Aircraft support the crossing of the Rhine.

APRIL 1945
29   Bomber Command drops food and supplies to Dutch people as part of Operation Manna.

MAY 1945
4   The first prisoners of war arrive back in the UK after being repatriated; 75,000 are returned by air.

8   Victory in Europe (VE) Day as Germany surrenders.

AUGUST 1945
15   Victory in Japan (VJ) Day as Japan surrenders.

STRENGTH
While Prime Minister Neville Chamberlain's efforts to prevent war had been a failure, they had bought some crucial time that allowed the RAF to strengthen. On the day war was declared, the air force had 11,753 officers and 163,939 other ranks. Fighter Command had 39 squadrons, 26 comprised of Spitfires or Hurricanes. Bomber Command had 25 operational squadrons based in the UK, equipped with Wellingtons, Blenheims, Whitleys and Hampdens.

STRUCTURE
At the beginning of the war the RAF in the UK was organised with the following commands:

- ▶ Fighter Command
- ▶ Bomber Command
- ▶ Coastal Command
- ▶ Training Command

- ▶ Maintenance Command

- ▶ Balloon Command

- ▶ Reserve Command.

Overseas there were three commands: Middle East, India and Far East.

With the need to expand, others were added later – Ferry Command (1941) and Transport Command (1943) – while Training Command was split into Flying Training and Technical Training.

WHEN THINGS DON'T GO RIGHT: THE BATTLE OF BARKING CREEK

Just days after war was declared in September 1939, Spitfires were scrambled to meet a suspected enemy raid. Two aircraft were shot down but the 'enemy' were in fact Hurricanes, and one pilot, Montague Hulton-Harrop, was killed. Two Spitfire pilots were court-martialled but cleared. The cause of the incident was a technical problem at a radar centre that confused a returning British aircraft with a German one. The incident led to a review of procedures.

NORWAY

On 9 April 1940 German forces invaded Norway and Denmark. The Danes offered little resistance but the Norwegians fought against the invaders. British and French troops landed and were supported by aircraft. Eighteen Gloster Gladiator biplanes of 263 Sqn made their base on a frozen lake, but all the aircraft were lost to enemy action, mechanical problems or were deliberately destroyed before evacuation. On 26 May the squadron returned with Hurricanes of 46 Sqn. They helped troops take Narvik, but the need for British forces was felt to be greater in France and on 7 June the squadrons were pulled out, with both Gladiators and Hurricanes landing on HMS *Glorious* – the Hurricanes having never attempted deck landings before. But the successful evacuation was in vain as the following day the carrier was sunk by German warships with the loss of 1,474 lives. Only two of the pilots who had landed survived. In Norway resistance to Nazi occupation ended two days later.

FRANCE

In 1939 aircraft were sent to France to attack German targets and to support British army units. The 'Phoney War' saw a period of relative inactivity that was shattered on 10 May 1940 when the Germans invaded the Low Countries and France. The air force suffered a high level of casualties. In one raid on 14 May against the German bridgehead at Sedan, 31 of the 71 aircraft were lost; 218 Sqn saw 90 per cent of its machines fail to return. The crews of the Fairey Battles, Bristol Blenheims and Hawker Hurricanes flew valiantly, but ultimately the German Blitzkrieg was too strong and the defending British and French forces too uncoordinated and unable to mount a strong enough defence. At the subsequent evacuation at Dunkirk the RAF mounted standing patrols over the beaches and further inland to allow as many ground personnel as possible to escape. Pilots and airmen later faced animosity from soldiers and sailors who asked 'Where were the RAF?' In fact, the air force flew 2,739 fighter sorties, 651 bomber sorties and 171 reconnaissance flights in the nine days of the evacuation.

'If we hadn't been there I don't think many of them would have got out.'
FLIGHT SERGEANT GEORGE UNWIN, SPITFIRE PILOT, 19 SQN

GREAT AIRCRAFT: HAWKER HURRICANE

Maximum speed: 339 mph*
Maximum altitude: 35,600 ft*
Armament: 4 x 20 mm cannon; 2 x 500 lb bombs*
Crew: 1

The Hurricane was the first RAF aircraft with retractable undercarriage and an enclosed cockpit. It arrived on squadrons in time to form the bulk of fighters in the Battle of Britain. Initially fitted with eight 0.303 inch calibre machine guns, some Hurricanes were fitted with 12 machine guns and others were equipped with four 20 mm cannons. The Hurricane was not as developed as the Spitfire and eventually became outdated as a day fighter against the later German marks of Me 109 and Focke-Wulf Fw 190. It continued to fly as a home defence night fighter and in the Burma and Desert War campaigns. In North Africa it played an important role as a 'tank buster'.

*Figures for Mark IIC.

THE BATTLE OF BRITAIN

The Battle of Britain began as a series of German raids on shipping and ports along the south coast of England in July 1940. The commander of Fighter Command, Air Chief Marshal Dowding, had prevented Spitfires from being based on the Continent earlier in the summer, aware that they were a finite resource and that to waste them in what he saw as a futile gesture of support for the doomed French was not something he was prepared to countenance. As it was, Fighter Command lost 477 fighters in May and June 1940 and, more importantly, 280 pilots who were killed.

As the summer wore on the raids became bigger and targets included RAF bases. Fighter Command came under increasing pressure but its morale remained high. The ability to resist the large bomber formations rested on the resupply of aircraft (both newly manufactured and repaired) as well as pilots. As much as possible, Dowding marshalled his resources, so that even at the height of the battle his squadrons were rotated out of the front line for a period to rest and replenish.

Some of the biggest aerial battles seen in warfare took place over south-east England as Hurricanes and Spitfires rose to meet wave after wave of Luftwaffe Heinkel, Junkers and Dornier bombers, as well as their Messerschmitt fighter escorts. By the end of September it was clear that Fighter Command had held firm as the Germans changed focus to attack London and threats of invasion diminished.

DID YOU KNOW?

A fifth of Fighter Command's aircrew during the battle came from non-UK countries: Australia, Belgium, Canada, Czechoslovakia, France, Ireland, Jamaica, New Zealand, Poland, Rhodesia, South Africa and the USA.

GREAT AIRCRAFT: VICKERS-SUPERMARINE SPITFIRE

Maximum speed: 454 mph*
Maximum altitude: 43,500 ft*
Armament: 4 x 20 mm cannon; rockets; or 1,000 lb of bombs*
Crew: 1

Designed by R. J. Mitchell, the Spitfire's handling and speed were much admired by pilots, and it was the only Allied aircraft in continuous production throughout the Second World War. German pilots shot down by Hurricanes insisted they were Spitfires. The Rolls-Royce Merlin engine powered the Spitfire through the early marks, but the engine power of its replacement, the Griffon, was double that of the early marks and the aircraft was some 35 per cent faster. Over 20,000 Spitfires were built for the air force.

*Figures for F.22 version

GREAT MEN OF THE AIR FORCE
HUGH DOWDING

Hugh Caswall Tremenheere Dowding joined the Royal Artillery in 1900 and the RFC in 1914. Known as 'Stuffy' for his aloof and unfriendly manner, he commanded a wing on the Western Front, but his real ability was as a staff officer. After the war he served overseas in Iraq and in 1926 was made Director of Training at the Air Ministry. He was promoted to Air Vice-Marshal, and then in the 1930s became Air Marshal. Heavily involved in developing the research and use of new equipment, when Fighter Command was created in 1936 Air Chief Marshal Dowding was put in charge. It was here he earned his place in history, organising the world's first co-ordinated air defence system utilising radar, observers, command centres and communications to assist the front-line fighter and anti-artillery units.

During the Battle of Britain Dowding faced criticism for being unable to resolve the dispute between 11 Group's commander, Keith Park, and 12 Group's commander, Trafford Leigh-Mallory, over the correct allocation of resources. This 'Big Wing' controversy overshadowed Dowding's success in the battle.

He was replaced in November 1940 and in 1943, on being awarded a barony, he chose his own Battle of Britain headquarters for his title: Baron Dowding of Bentley Priory. He died in 1970.

THE BOMBING CAMPAIGN

*'The fighters are our salvation but the bombers alone
provide the means of victory.'*
**PRIME MINISTER WINSTON CHURCHILL TO HIS WAR CABINET,
3 SEPTEMBER 1940**

Bomber Command was in action on the very first day of the war, sending a Blenheim on a reconnaissance mission. It spotted German warships which were attacked the next day.

Early bombing raids were not hugely successful, with poor navigation and low bombing accuracy. The casualty rate was high: in one attack on Wilhelmshaven in December 1939, 12 Wellingtons were shot down out of the 24 that set out. German radar had alerted anti-aircraft guns and aircraft.

These daylight raids were soon abandoned but the switch to night-time operations saw a reduction in navigation and bombing accuracy. Targets near to coasts were selected as these were easier to navigate towards.

After the setbacks on land of 1940, the bomber was seen as the only way to carry the war to Germany. Industrial targets were attacked but bombers were to avoid inflicting civilian casualties. However, following the Butt Report of August 1941, which highlighted the poor accuracy of the RAF's bombing – only one in four aircraft attacking targets in Germany had managed to drop bombs within 5 miles of their target – the strategy was changed and 'area bombing', the targeting of cities, was introduced. It was believed that this would lead to a collapse of morale and resultant German defeat.

In February 1942 a new commander took over – Arthur Harris – whose nickname 'Bomber' came from his firm belief that the bomber would win the war. He oversaw the bombing of Lübeck in March 1942, which saw most of the old part of the city destroyed; Rostock was also heavily hit. The RAF's bombers were able to use new equipment such as GEE, which aided navigation, and at the end of May 1942 the first 1,000-bomber raid took place when 1,047 aircraft, collected from

52 airfields and included training units, attacked the city of Cologne. Although 40 aircraft were lost, Harris claimed the mission as a notable success and a boost for morale, though Bomber Command did not have the resources to continue with raids in such numbers.

GREAT MEN OF THE AIR FORCE ARTHUR HARRIS

'There are a lot of people who say that bombing can never win a war. Well, my answer to that is that it has never been tried yet and we shall see.'
AIR MARSHAL SIR ARTHUR HARRIS, 1942

There are few figures more controversial in the history of the air force than Arthur Harris. He had flown night fighters in the First World War and remained in the service post-war, commanding squadrons in India and Iraq. During the 1930s Harris was a staff officer in the Air Ministry, where he advocated the procurement of long-range bombers. After war began he took charge of a bomber group and then in 1942 was appointed in the role that was to make him the figure of so much public debate. Harris was focused on what he believed was the correct course. He did not instigate the policy of area bombing but he did believe that heavy attritional aerial attack would wear down the German population's appetite for continuing the war. Hardworking, determined and single-minded, Harris came in for much criticism but also earned the respect of his staff and crews for backing them in what was a dangerous endeavour.

GREAT AIRCRAFT: AVRO LANCASTER

Maximum speed:	287 mph
Maximum altitude:	24,500 ft
Armament:	8 x 0.303 inch machine guns; up to a 22,000 lb bombload
Crew:	7

A major factor in the renewed bombing campaign after 1941 was the Avro Lancaster. It could carry heavier bombloads for further distances than previous bomber types and Lancasters bore the brunt of the British strategic bombing offensive. Its effectiveness was shown in the statistic that for every Lancaster lost in action, 132 tons of bombs were dropped. For the Handley Page Halifax the figure was less than half that – just 56 tons. By March 1945, 56 front-line squadrons had Lancasters. From the 7,000 built only one continues to fly in the UK, as part of the Battle of Britain Memorial Flight.

POINTBLANK

In January 1943 a meeting took place between Winston Churchill and American President Franklin D. Roosevelt, along with their respective air staff officers, as a result of which the Casablanca Directive was issued to both the British and American air forces. In Operation Pointblank, they were to pursue:

> '... *the progressive destruction and dislocation of the*
> *German military, industrial and economic system,*
> *and the undermining of the morale of the German*
> *people to a point where their capacity for armed*
> *resistance is fatally weakened'.*

The American bombers would carry out daylight raids, with their counterparts operating at night. Bombers received help through the Pathfinder Force (formed in August 1942), which marked targets with flares for the approaching bomber force. This and electronic aids such as GEE and Oboe, which used beams sent from the UK, led to greater accuracy, while airborne radar (H2S) also helped navigators determine their location and the target.

As the bombing offensive intensified, aircrew casualties resulted as the Germans improved their aerial defences, with radar-guided night fighters and anti-aircraft guns.

Bomber Command responded with countermeasures, using 'Window' – strips of aluminium which when dropped confused the defenders' radar picture. This was first used in the attacks on Hamburg at the end of July 1943, when the dry weather combined with the incendiaries dropped caused a firestorm that is estimated to have killed 40,000 people. After the Battle of Hamburg, attention was then focused on Berlin.

BATTLE OF BERLIN

The Battle of Berlin which began in the summer of 1943 was to prove extremely difficult. The German capital was farther away and air defences were improved. The battle continued through to March 1944 but loss rates were high (a third of all Bomber Command's operational deaths during the war occurred in the year following September 1943) and operationally it was not a success. The city was spread out and less susceptible to sustained damage.

Then at the end of March 1944 the city of Nuremberg was selected for a large raid. It was a disaster: 95 aircraft were lost, almost 12 per cent of those that took off. The bright moon allowed the Luftwaffe's night fighters to make repeated attacks.

Despite Harris's objections, bombers were moved to concentrate on targets in preparation for the D-Day landings in June 1944 and also to hit the V1 and V2 rocket sites with the greater accuracy that was now possible. In September 1944 Harris resumed the offensive on German cities and on the night of 13/14 February 1945, American and British bombers attacked the city of Dresden as part of Operation Thunderclap, the plan to hit cities in the east of Germany to assist the Soviet army's advance. The bomber offensive continued through to the war's end in May 1945.

LOSSES

Operational: 47,130
Non-operational: 8,090

As POWs: 138
Other causes: 215
Total: 55,573

In the course of the war, 125,000 men flew in Bomber Command, so the loss rate of more than 44 per cent was unrivalled by any other branch of the British armed forces during the war. The effectiveness of the bombing offensive has remained a topic for debate. Despite Harris's request, no campaign medal was awarded for the crews of Bomber Command.

> '*We must never forget that all the time, night after night, month after month, our bomber squadrons travel far into Germany, find their targets in the darkness by the highest navigational skill, aim their attacks, often under the heaviest fire, often with serious loss, with deliberate careful discrimination, and inflict shattering blows upon the whole of the technical and war-making structure of the Nazi power.*'
> **WINSTON CHURCHILL, 20 AUGUST 1940, HOUSES OF PARLIAMENT**

GREAT MEN OF THE AIR FORCE
GUY GIBSON

Gibson joined the air force in 1936 and when war began flew Handley Page Hampdens before becoming a night fighter pilot flying the Bristol Beaufighter with 29 Sqn. He shot down four enemy aircraft. Then in April 1942 Gibson was given command of 106 Sqn, operating the Lancaster. He remained with the unit until March 1943, by which time it was regarded as the best bomber squadron in 5 Group.

Gibson's next posting was to earn him legendary status. He was given command of a newly established squadron, which was formed to carry out a secret mission that was only revealed to its commander and crews close to the date of the operation: to drop a specially designed weapon on the Ruhr dams. Gibson's leadership and personal bravery, in flying alongside other Lancasters to draw fire while they made their low-level bomb runs, earned him a Victoria Cross.

After the raid he took part in publicity work across the Atlantic and wrote a memoir called Enemy Coast Ahead. But his yearning to return to operations saw him take part in a raid on 19/20 September 1944 in which his Mosquito crashed on the way home and Gibson was killed. He was 26 years old.

GREAT AIRCRAFT: DE HAVILLAND MOSQUITO

Maximum speed: 380 mph*
Maximum altitude: 36,000 ft*
Armament: 4 x 20 mm cannon, 4 x 0.303 inch machine
                   guns, 4 x 500 lb bombs*
Crew: 2

In 1937 Bomber Command had expressed the need for a fast bomber able to outrun enemy fighters. De Havilland was given the task of producing such a machine and on 25 November 1940 the first flight took place of an aircraft that was to earn its place in air force history. The Mosquito had two Rolls-Royce Merlin engines and because of its wooden construction was light and therefore fast. It was used in a number of roles: bombing, target marking, reconnaissance, maritime strikes and as a night fighter. Mosquitoes made low-level precision attacks on Amiens prison and Gestapo HQs in Norway, Netherlands and Denmark. The last front-line operational sortie took place on 15 December 1955 in a PR.34 flying in Singapore.

*Figures for FB.VI version.

GREAT MEN OF THE AIR FORCE
LEONARD CHESHIRE

Leonard Cheshire flew the Armstrong Whitworth Whitley bomber at the start of the war, before moving onto Halifaxes. By April 1941 he had been awarded the Distinguished Flying Cross (DFC) and the Distinguished Service Order (DSO) and bar, and had reached the rank of Flight Lieutenant. His first DSO was for bringing his crew home after their aircraft had been shot up and set on fire.

In April 1943 Cheshire became the youngest man to reach the rank of Group Captain, aged 25, taking charge of Marston Moor airfield in North Yorkshire. However he wished to return to combat duties and reverted to the lower rank of Wing Commander to take over 617 Sqn in September 1943. He instigated new low-level target-marking techniques and flew a single-engined Mustang to perform pathfinding duties as Master Bomber in a raid on a V2 rocket storage site. Cheshire was awarded the VC in September 1944. In August 1945 he was a British observer at Nagasaki, but in 1946 he left the air force with mental health issues. He set up the Cheshire Foundation Homes for the severely disabled and devoted the rest of his life to providing care for those less fortunate than himself.

SECOND WORLD WAR AIR FORCE SLANG

ack-ack	Anti-aircraft artillery fire. The phonetic alphabet used 'ack' for 'A'
Archie	Anti-aircraft artillery fire. The origin of the term stems from the First World War when a crew were over enemy territory when they came under fire. Each time they avoided a burst they sang a music hall song of the time: 'Archibald, Certainly Not!' and the shortened form of the man's name became widely used
bounce	Surprise attack on a formation flying below
the deck	The ground

dicing	Flying low-level photo-reconnaissance sorties
the drink	The sea
erk	Member of the ground crew
gardening	Laying mines
jankers	Menial chores, given as punishment
kite	An aircraft
shooting a line	Telling an exaggerated story
snappers	Me 109 fighters
squirt	Short burst of machine-gun fire

CLOSE AIR SUPPORT

During the desert campaign of 1940–42, the RAF gained great experience in the tactical use of air power in conjunction with ground forces. In the subsequent campaign in Italy the Allies achieved air superiority, and a 'cab rank' system was operated whereby orbiting fighters could be called down by forward air controllers to attack enemy positions. This was continued in north-west Europe with Spitfires and Typhoons of the Second Allied Tactical Air Force (2ATAF) commanded by Air Marshal Arthur Coningham, who had led the Desert Air Force. Heavy bombers targeted railways, radar stations and armaments factories in France, but the fighters roamed the skies looking for trains, troop convoys or other targets of opportunity. As well as its four 20 mm cannon, the Hawker Typhoon could carry eight unguided rockets, which provided devastating firepower. One of the reasons behind the failure of the Arnhem airborne operation was that faults with the radios of the airborne troops prevented close air support being called in.

THE BATTLE OF THE ATLANTIC

The Battle of the Atlantic saw the ships and aircraft of the navy and the RAF's Coastal Command attempt to counter the German U-boats threatening supplies being shipped from across the Atlantic. At the start of the war Coastal Command's aircraft lacked range, weaponry and detection equipment, but in the face of mounting shipping losses, improvements came in the shape of longer-ranged machines such as the Liberator, Sunderland and Catalina; aerial depth charges; and air-to-surface vessel radar. By the war's end Coastal Command had sunk 192 U-boats and, while the cost of 5,863 aircrew was high, the price of losing the lifeline of supplies from North America would have been incalculable.

AIRCREW NICKNAMES

The tradition of pilots and navigators being given nicknames is long established. These are some from the Second World War:

Arty	Sergeant Pilot Ray T. Holmes
Bogle	Pilot Officer Crelin Bodie
Bubble	Flying Officer Robin McGregor Waterston
Bunny	Wing Commander Christopher F. Currant
Cocky	Flying Officer Hugh S. L. Dundas
Grubby	Pilot Officer Douglas H. Grice
Grumpy	Flight Sergeant George C. Unwin
Laddie	Wing Commander Percy B. Lucas
Raspberry	Pilot Officer R. Berry
Shovel	Squadron Leader Terence G. Lovell-Gregg
Social Type Jeff	Pilot Officer Geoffrey N. Gaunt
Sleepy	Pilot Officer G. W. Walker
Sticky	Squadron Leader Norman V. Glew
Tubby	Squadron Leader Herbert W. Mermagen
Weasel	Flying Officer Patrick Woods-Scawen
Wombat	Pilot Officer C. A. 'Tony' Woods-Scawen

SOUTH EAST ASIA

On 15 February 1942 Britain's armed forces surrendered to the Japanese at Singapore in what was described by Winston Churchill as the 'worst disaster'. The Japanese invasion of Malaya had been met with inadequate air assets: the Brewster Buffalo was no match for the Japanese Zero, and the Allies were outnumbered and not well organised. Japanese forces then moved on Burma and despite resistance from Hurricanes, Blenheims and P-40 Tomahawks, the advance continued.

Transport aircraft carried supplies over the eastern Himalayas into China on a route known as 'the Hump'. A Japanese offensive into India was met with heavy fighting at Imphal and Kohima in 1944. The air supply operation to Commonwealth troops dropped 400 tons a day. Orde Wingate's Chindits, operating hundreds of miles behind enemy lines, were supplied by air and wounded men were airlifted out.

Ground attack aircraft utilised the 'cab rank' system and helped the advancing forces gain the upper hand in the successful land offensive in Burma that saw Japanese forces pushed back.

SUMMARY

The RAF had operated in all theatres of the war, whether it be jungle, desert, over the sea or closer to home. It had been forced to expand. In July 1944 it had over 1.1 million men and women in uniform and by the war's end almost 480 airfields. It had developed great advances in technological areas such as airborne radar, radar-aided bombing, photo reconnaissance and engine power – including the revolutionary introduction of jet power.

CHAPTER FOUR

BEYOND THE SECOND WORLD WAR

TIMELINE

JUNE 1948

24   Soviet Union closes land routes to Berlin, leading to the Berlin Airlift.

JULY 1948

Aircraft begin supporting the counter-insurgency campaign in Malaya.

14   Six Vampires of 54 Sqn make the first jet crossings of the Atlantic.

JANUARY 1949

7   Four RAF Spitfires are shot down by Israeli Spitfires and anti-aircraft fire in a confrontation between Israel and Egypt.

FEBRUARY 1949

1   Women's Royal Air Force (WRAF) established.

OCTOBER 1949

6   Last flight into Berlin as part of airlift.

JUNE 1950

25   North Korean forces invade South Korea.

APRIL 1952

RAF crews fly secret overflight reconnaissance missions over the Soviet Union to gain information on potential target sites.

SEPTEMBER 1952

20   WRAF Volunteer Reserve Pilot Officer Jean Lennox Bird becomes the first British woman to be presented with pilot's wings.

OCTOBER 1952

3   The UK explodes its first atomic bomb.

MARCH 1953

12   An Avro Lincoln bomber is shot down by a MiG 15 after it strays into Soviet-controlled airspace over Germany. Seven aircrew are killed.

JULY 1953

27   An armistice ends the Korean War.

NOVEMBER 1953

11   The first Lincoln bombers arrive in Kenya and are the first deployment against Mau Mau insurgents in a campaign that lasts until 1955.

OCTOBER 1956

11 The first atomic bomb to be dropped by a British aircraft (Valiant) is tested in South Australia.

31 Canberras and Valiants attack Egyptian airfields as part of Operation Musketeer.

NOVEMBER 1957

8 Britain explodes its first hydrogen bomb at Christmas Island.

JULY 1960

31 The Malayan Emergency is declared over. Air force aircraft have flown over 375,000 sorties during the campaign.

JULY 1961

1 Aircraft begin to be deployed to Kuwait as part of Operation Vantage.

JANUARY 1962

1 Bomber Command begins keeping its nuclear-armed V-bombers on quick reaction alert (QRA).

OCTOBER 1962

26 The Cuban Missile Crisis sees nuclear bombers and missile squadrons on the highest alert.

DECEMBER 1962

8 Indonesian-backed forces attempt to take control of Brunei in northern Borneo.

JANUARY 1964

4 Operation Nutcracker begins in which the RAF flies missions in support of the army in Aden.

AUGUST 1966

11   The Indonesian Confrontation ends as Indonesia recognises Malaysia.

NOVEMBER 1967

29   The last British military personnel are airlifted out of Aden.

APRIL 1968

5   Flight Lieutenant Alan Pollock of 1(F) Sqn flies his Hunter through Tower Bridge in protest at what he felt were insufficient celebrations of the RAF's 50th anniversary.

30   Strike Command is created, absorbing Bomber and Fighter Commands. Coastal Command joins them the following year.

JUNE 1969

30   The navy takes over operation of Britain's nuclear deterrent.

JULY 1974

20   An airlift from Cyprus begins following the Turkish invasion of the island. Some 22,000 people are eventually flown out.

APRIL 1982

2   Argentinian forces invade the Falkland Islands.

30   The first raid of Operation Black Buck sees a Vulcan bomber set a long-distance bombing record in attacking Port Stanley airfield.

MAY 1982

20   Harrier GR.3s fly their first combat sorties, attacking a fuel dump.

JUNE 1982

14   Argentinian forces surrender.

OCTOBER 1982

17   The first Phantoms arrive at Port Stanley for air defence duties.

SEPTEMBER 1983

Buccaneers fly at low level over Beirut to indicate preparedness to defend the British Consulate during the Lebanese Civil War.

AUGUST 1990

2   Iraq invades Kuwait.

11   The first British aircraft deploy to the Persian Gulf as part of the UK response to the Iraqi invasion of Kuwait.

JANUARY 1991

17   Tornadoes take part in the first bombing missions of the Gulf War.

SEPTEMBER 1991

Jaguars begin Operation Warden, enforcing a UN No Fly Zone over northern Iraq.

AUGUST 1992

Tornadoes begin Operation Jural, enforcing a UN No Fly Zone over southern Iraq.

APRIL 1993

As part of a NATO force, British aircraft take part in Operation Deny Flight over Bosnia.

APRIL 1994

1   The WRAF disbands.

JUNE 1994

2   A Chinook ZD576 crashes on the Mull of Kintyre, killing all 29 people on board.

AUGUST 1994

The first female fast-jet pilot, Jo Salter, joins 617 Sqn.

AUGUST 1995

30   British aircraft begin flying missions as part of Operation Deliberate Force against Serbian forces in Bosnia.

MARCH 1999

24/25   British aircraft begin flying missions as part of Operation Allied Force against Serbian forces in Kosovo.

SEPTEMBER 2000

10   Chinooks take part in a rescue mission of British troops in Sierra Leone.

OCTOBER 2001

7   Following the 9/11 attacks, British aircraft join American forces in combat operations in Afghanistan. Their actions later form part of Operation Herrick.

MARCH 2003

19   British aircraft take part in Operation Telic, the invasion of Iraq.

MARCH 2004

NATO begins air policing in the Baltic area following Estonia, Latvia and Lithuania's entry into NATO. Tornado F.3s are the first UK fighters to take part.

MARCH 2011

22/23   British Typhoons carry out their first-ever combat sorties as part of Operation Ellamy over Libya.

DECEMBER 2014

NATO ends its combat operations in Afghanistan.

OCTOBER 2015

4 Air force Search and Rescue operations end with the final sortie of 22 Sqn's Sea Kings.

DECEMBER 2015

2 The UK Parliament votes to permit British combat sorties against Islamic State of Iraq and the Levant (ISIL).

INTRODUCTION

The RAF ended the Second World War with over 55,000 aircraft, of which 9,200 were in the front line. Over a million men and women were in uniform but, as with the aftermath of the First World War, the service was to face huge reductions in inventory and personnel. By 1949 it had less than 220,000 personnel, but the reduced force was not to enjoy a sustained period of post-war peace, as it faced the first 'battle' in what was to be known as the Cold War.

Berlin Airlift

Winston Churchill had warned of the threat of the Soviet Union soon after the war ended, referring in 1946 to the 'Iron Curtain' which had descended across the continent of Europe. In 1948 the Soviets began a process of cutting off access to Berlin, in an attempt to force the Allies to leave. The German capital was situated 100 miles inside Soviet-controlled territory and was administered by the former wartime Allies of the Soviet Union, France, the USA and the UK.

In June the Soviets closed all rail and road routes into the city. The only route in was by air, along three corridors, 20 miles wide, to two German airfields: Gatow and Tempelhof. On 24 June an airlift by Allied air forces began to supply the two million Berliners and the Allied garrison with food, coal and other supplies. It was thought the operation would only last a few weeks, but in fact it lasted for nearly 11 months, with the blockade being lifted only on 12 May 1949, although flights continued until September.

Transport Command used Douglas Dakotas, Avro Yorks and Handley Page Hastings, while Coastal Command flew Sunderland flying boats to the city's Havel Lake. Civilian aircraft were also chartered. At its height an aircraft landed every minute and by the end the RAF had delivered over 352,000 tons of cargo in 65,857 missions, and it had also flown out over 35,000 passengers. But it came at a price for the RAF, as 18 aircrew were killed in accidents.

DID YOU KNOW?

The Berlin Airlift began as Operation Knicker. Then for a short while it was renamed Carter Paterson until it was pointed out that this was the name of a British removals company. As this gave the wrong impression, it was swiftly changed again, this time to Operation Plainfare.

GREAT AIRCRAFT: GLOSTER METEOR

Maximum speed: 590 mph*
Maximum altitude: 44,000 ft*
Armament: 4 x 20 mm cannon*
Crew: 1
*Figures for F.8 version.

The Meteor was the RAF's first operational jet aircraft, entering service in 1944 with 616 Sqn. It was used to defend UK airspace against the V1 flying bombs and on 4 August a Meteor brought down a V1 by tipping it over when the aircraft's guns jammed. Meteors also operated in north-west Europe during the last weeks of the war. After the war they were the RAF's main jet day fighter until the introduction of the Hawker Hunter. Meteors were operated by the Royal Australian Air Force and were the only British-made jet fighter to see action in the Korean War. As they were withdrawn from front-line service, the Meatbox, as it was known, served in training, target-tug and reconnaissance roles.

DID YOU KNOW?

Soon after the Second World War ended the air force re-formed its High Speed Flight to set new speed records. It had been created in the 1920s to take part in the Schneider Trophy races, which were won outright by the United Kingdom in 1931. In its post-war guise the flight set a new record in September 1946 of 615.8 mph in a Gloster Meteor.

Malaya

With the war at an end, the peace did not last long. In 1948 Hawker Tempests flew sorties against tribes in Somaliland and attacked guerrilla bases held by the Shifta bandits in Eritrea, but it was in South East Asia that the RAF became involved in a long-running campaign. Unrest in Malaya resulted in planters being killed and a state of emergency was called in 1948. In July the UK sent Spitfires, Dakotas and Mosquitoes, and elements of the RAF Regiment. The 'Malayan Emergency', as it was termed, saw the air force increase its strength, with Beaufighters, Vampires, Meteors, Sunderlands and Lincolns all being deployed. They carried out reconnaissance, troop-carrying missions, leaflet drops, aerial broadcasts and supply drops amounting to 25,000 tons.

Close air support missions took place, but were reduced in number as the jungle terrain made them ineffective. Helicopters were involved in a new role: casualty evacuation or 'casevac'. Westland Dragonflies and Bristol Sycamores were used, and Dragonflies were also used as ad-hoc gunships, with troops carrying Bren guns.

Malaya became independent in 1957 but the insurgency carried on until 1960 when the state of emergency was ended. In total, 76 air force personnel died in the conflict.

DID YOU KNOW?

The RAF flew combat missions in Vietnam. Following the defeat of Japan in 1945 the Viet Minh, led by Ho Chi Minh, attempted to seize control of the country. This was resisted by France, and British Spitfires and Mosquitoes flew missions in support of French forces. The British needed additional resources and so enlisted their recently defeated foe, the Japanese, who operated their own transport aircraft in a unit called the Gremlin Task Force.

Korea

The Korean War was the first 'hot war' of the Cold War, beginning in 1950 when communist North Korea attacked the South and the United Nations sent forces to defend it. The only air force aircraft that took part were Short Sunderlands which carried out maritime patrols. However, over 50 British pilots flew with the Royal Australian Air Force (RAAF) and the United States Air Force (USAF), of whom nine were killed. Those flying with the USAF flew Sabres and accounted for several MiG 15 fighters. The RAAF flew Meteors which were outclassed by the MiGs.

DID YOU KNOW?

In July 1953 to mark the Queen's Coronation, a special event was held at RAF Odiham in Hampshire at which over 300 aircraft were arranged for inspection by the Queen. A fly-past saw 640 aircraft take part. In 2012, to mark the Queen's Diamond Jubilee, 87 aircraft took part in a fly-past at Windsor Castle.

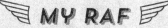 MY RAF

DANIEL FERGUSON
Leading Aircraftman, served 1951–53

The initial training at Padgate was terrifying but necessary. Technical training came later on, at Kirkham, which was much better. I applied for aircrew at Hornchurch, to be an observer/air gunner, and was accepted, but they required me to sign on as a regular for an extra three years after I passed the examination

After the first six weeks I really enjoyed my service period and took greater pride in myself and the RAF. I was involved in a period of selection and training for the Queen's Coronation in June 1953. We drilled for six weeks in preparation. In the end only one of our group actually got to go to London. However, we paraded in the county town, Taunton, which was a very proud moment for our squad and a strong memory for me. One of the most memorable characters I remember was Station Warrant Officer Horrobin at armament training at Watchet in Somerset. He was a great help to me and was a great leader of his men.

I served on three stations as an armament mechanic and I remember a single Beaufighter pulling a drogue across the sky at Watchet, which the RAF Regiment attempted to shoot down with the Bofors anti-aircraft gun. They were given a certain amount of encouragement from the onlookers!

After my national service I was placed on reserve and was posted on three occasions for further training at Leuchars with 43 Sqn which was handy, being less than 20 miles away from my home town.

Suez

When Egypt's President Nasser nationalised the Suez Canal in July 1956, France and the United Kingdom organised a military response, in conjunction with Israel. Operation Musketeer saw a force of over 420 French and UK aircraft deployed, including Venoms, Canberras, Hunters, Meteors, Valettas, Hastings and Valiants. Bombing against Egyptian airfields began on 31 October. But international pressure grew quickly and by 4 November bombing had stopped. A ceasefire followed several days later.

Kuwait

In a forerunner of a future and larger operation, in 1961 a rapid deployment of ground troops and RAF aircraft was made to counter Iraq's claims on Kuwaiti territory. The crisis was averted and all British assets were redeployed without being used in action.

Aden

In 1958 British aircraft had been called into action in support of the army against Yemeni forces, but it was the 1960s that saw a large deployment of aircraft and personnel at Khormaksar. A republican coup in neighbouring Yemen in 1962 increased anti-British feeling in the area. Hunters and Shackletons were engaged in combat activity. As insurgent activity increased, the British government announced in 1964 that Aden would be granted independence and a large airlift removed the last British personnel in November 1967.

GREAT AIRCRAFT: HAWKER HUNTER

Maximum speed:	715 mph*
Maximum altitude:	51,500 ft*
Armament:	4 x 30 mm cannon, 2 x 500 lb bombs or 100-gallon Napalm tanks or rockets*
Crew:	1

The Hunter was the air force's main day jet fighter during the 1950s and was well regarded by its pilots. It first entered service as an interceptor, but later marks were used in ground attack and reconnaissance roles. In 1958 111 Sqn led 22 Hunters in a world record formation loop at the Farnborough Airshow.

*Figures for F.6 version.

Indonesian Confrontation

When Indonesia began sending guerrillas into northern Borneo in 1963 it started a conflict known as the Indonesian Confrontation. The air force was heavily involved, utilising transport aircraft such as the Beverley, Hastings, Valetta, Twin Pioneer and Argosy. Bristol Belvedere and Westland Whirlwind helicopters were used for airlifting troops and evacuating injured personnel. Hunters and Javelins were deployed, with Canberras for reconnaissance and Shackletons for maritime patrol. The conflict changed in nature in 1964 with incursions into Malaysia by Indonesian troops, and ground attack sorties were launched by the RAF. Victor bombers were also sent to act as a deterrent, and the confrontation ended in 1966 with a peace treaty between Indonesia and Malaysia.

GREAT AIRCRAFT: ENGLISH ELECTRIC CANBERRA

Maximum speed:	580 mph*
Maximum altitude:	48,000 ft*
Armament:	No defensive armament, bomber versions: 6,000 lb bombload and the interdictor version carried a gun pack
Crew:	2

*Figures for PR.7 version.

The Canberra was the UK's first jet bomber. It first flew in 1949 and was delivered two years later. It was designed as a fast, light bomber to replace the de Havilland Mosquito, and its versatility saw it operate in different roles as a tactical nuclear bomber, interdictor, trainer, target tug and in the photo-reconnaissance role, in the last of which it served until retirement in 2006.

NUCLEAR DETERRENT

'The answer to an atomic bomb on London is an atomic bomb on another great city.'
PRIME MINISTER CLEMENT ATTLEE, MEMORANDUM, 29 AUGUST 1945

Following the American use of atomic bombs on Japan in 1945, it was felt that the United Kingdom should develop its own nuclear weapons. Approval was given in 1947 and within five years, the first test explosion had taken place. Air force aircraft carried the weapons, firstly freefall bombs such as Blue Danube and Yellow Sun, and later the Blue Steel stand-off missile. Three different aircraft entered air force service as part of the V-bomber force: the Vickers Valiant, Avro Vulcan and Handley Page Victor. Crews were placed on quick reaction alert (QRA), ready to take off in the face of an imminent attack – the famous 'four-minute warning' – and dispersed operations were planned at 36 airfields in the UK to reduce the chances of a successful Soviet first strike attack. Then in 1969 the navy was given responsibility for the UK's nuclear deterrent, with the Polaris intercontinental ballistic missile (ICBM) system launched from its nuclear-powered submarines. The RAF retained nuclear weapons until 1998 when the WE.177 tactical nuclear bomb was withdrawn from service.

GREAT AIRCRAFT: AVRO VULCAN

Maximum speed:	645 mph
Maximum altitude:	60,000 ft
Armament:	No defensive armament.
	Offensive armament: nuclear weapon or 21 x 1,000 lb bombs.
Crew:	5

The Avro Vulcan was the world's first delta-winged jet bomber. It first flew in August 1952 and performed at the Farnborough Airshow soon afterwards. It was at Farnborough where test pilot Roly Falk famously rolled the giant delta. Vulcans were designed for nuclear bombing but, ironically, it was as a conventional bomber that it entered aviation history with its long-range endurance bombing missions in the Falklands conflict of 1982. Soon afterwards, Vulcans were converted to aerial tankers before being retired from operational service in 1984.

DID YOU KNOW?

In order to show the long-range potential of the V-bomber force, a Vulcan flew non-stop from the UK to Australia in 1961. It took 20 hours and 5 minutes, being refuelled four times.

COLD WAR ACRONYMS

COLPRO   Collective protection shelter
FWOC   Forward wing operations centre
HAS   Hardened aircraft shelter
MAXEVAL   Maximum evaluation
MINIVAL   Minimum evaluation
NADGE   NATO Air Defence Ground Environment
NBC   Nuclear, biological and chemical
SACEUR   Supreme Allied Commander Europe
TACEVAL   Tactical evaluation
WREBUS   Weapons research establishment break-up system

COLD WAR EXERCISES

With the Cold War at its height during the 1980s, units often carried out exercises to improve their readiness. RAF squadrons trained with their NATO counterparts in scenarios made as realistic as possible to prepare them for any potential conflict with the Soviet Union. Exercises were given codenames such as Brilliant Invader, Northern Merger or Cheerful Challenge, some of which might appear incongruous to the serious intentions of those taking part.

ELINT OPERATIONS

Electronic intelligence (ELINT) operations were flown during the Second World War to gather information on German radar and communications, and this was continued against the Soviet Union. Flights codenamed 'Ferret' were flown close to the Soviet Union's borders from 1948, and these secret missions were continued under the guise of 'radar calibration' or 'radio proving flights'. Canberras and Comets were used and in 1975 the Nimrod R.1s of 51 Sqn took on the role until the type's withdrawal in 2011. The Boeing RC-135W Rivet Joint was received in 2013 to carry out this role.

QRA

Fighters stationed in the UK were tasked with providing continuous air defence cover. Quick reaction alert (QRA) Lightning, Phantom and then Tornado F.3 aircraft were kept armed, fuelled and ready to go at 10 minutes' readiness to get airborne. (In Germany aircraft tasked with the same role, known as Battle Flight, had a target of 5 minutes to get airborne.) Aircrews would be on alert for 24-hour periods (with ground crew stationed for longer), ready to take off when the air defence radars picked up any aircraft inbound towards UK airspace. Northern Q was provided by Leuchars and Southern Q by Coningsby, Wattisham and Binbrook. Following the end of the Soviet Union, this role was reduced. Its function is now provided by Typhoons from Lossiemouth and Coningsby.

GREAT AIRCRAFT: ENGLISH ELECTRIC LIGHTNING

Maximum speed:	1,500 mph*
Maximum altitude:	60,000 ft plus*
Armament:	2 x Red Top or Firestreak AAM missiles.
	2 x 30 mm cannon in ventral pack.*
Crew:	1

The Lightning replaced the Hunter as Britain's main day interceptor during the 1960s. Featuring an unusual engine layout of two Rolls-Royce Avons mounted with one above the other, it was renowned for its rapid acceleration and climbing performance. It was the first British aircraft to achieve supersonic speed in level flight and was the UK's first Mach 2-capable fighter. The Lightning was well liked by its pilots, who admired its power and manoeuvrability, but a failure to upgrade the avionics hampered its abilities as an interceptor and its fuel consumption rate was such that the pilot always had one eye on the fuel gauge. The RAF's last all-British fighter was retired from service in 1988.

*Figures for F.6 version.

DID YOU KNOW?

Former Lightning pilots are known as WIWOLS, which stands for how they begin their anecdotes: 'When I was on Lightnings…'

WHEN THINGS DON'T GO RIGHT: F-4 SHOOTS DOWN JAGUAR

During the Cold War air defence crews trained rigorously in the procedures and tactics that would be used in a 'hot war'. In Germany Phantoms would regularly fly with live weapons. During an exercise in May 1982 a Phantom from 92 Sqn claimed a unique place in air force history. Carrying out a practice interception on a Jaguar from 14 Sqn the pilot selected the heat-seeking Sidewinder and when he pressed the weapon's release he was surprised to see the actual missile speed away from under his wing. An urgent radio call to the Jaguar pilot from his flight leader ensured his swift ejection and parachute descent. The reasons behind the inadvertent shooting down were put down to the Phantom's armed status not being properly indicated in the cockpit or checked by ground controllers.

SEARCH AND RESCUE

One of the more familiar of air force aircraft in the post-war era was the yellow helicopter carrying out the search and rescue (SAR) role. During the Second World War downed aircrew were picked up from the sea by rescue launches and Supermarine Walrus amphibians, while Westland Lysanders and Avro Ansons dropped dinghies. The larger Vickers Warwicks and Lockheed Hudsons dropped life rafts big enough for a whole bomber crew. Pigeons were used by downed crews to alert rescue services of their predicament.

The first operational SAR helicopter squadron was 275 Sqn, flying Bristol Sycamores, in 1953. It was followed in this role by the Westland Whirlwind and the Wessex and then the Sea King, which flew these often hazardous flights in the UK's coastal and mountainous areas. The air force's SAR function was replaced by that of the Bristow Group in 2015. The yellow helicopters worked closely with the RAF Mountain Rescue Service, which has three teams of volunteers and permanent staff based at Lossiemouth, Leeming and Valley.

DID YOU KNOW?

Lawrence of Arabia played an important part in the rescue service. Following his exploits in the desert, T. E. Lawrence enlisted in the air force in an attempt to escape his fame. He joined the Marine Section in 1925 as 'T. E. Shaw', and after witnessing a fatal seaplane crash worked on developing faster rescue boats for picking up downed aircrew.

THE FALKLANDS CONFLICT

The air force in the early 1980s was configured for a potential conventional war with Warsaw Pact forces on the battleground of mainland Europe; it was thought likely to escalate quickly into a nuclear conflict. But this planning was quickly set aside in the spring of 1982 when Argentina invaded the Falkland Islands and Britain decided on a military solution.

A naval task force was put together with two aircraft carriers: HMS *Invincible* and HMS *Hermes*. Both were equipped with the Sea Harrier, a naval version of the Harrier ground attack V/STOL (vertical/short take-off and landing) aircraft. Although capable, it did not have the armament, endurance and radar of other fighters. Seven RAF pilots were assigned to the Fleet Air Arm and flying Sea Harriers when the task force sailed.

Operation Corporate involved extensive air force participation. Aircraft were based on Ascension Island, which served as a staging post. Nimrod maritime reconnaissance aircraft, C-130 and VC10 transporters, Victor tankers and Vulcan bombers were all based there during the conflict. The latter were involved in one of the most memorable actions of the war.

Black Buck 1

On 30 April two Vulcans took off from Ascension, loaded with 21,000 lb of freefall bombs. The lead aircraft had a faulty window seal and couldn't pressurise properly, so the reserve aircraft XM607, piloted by Flight Lieutenant Martin Withers, took over.

The target was Port Stanley airfield, 3,886 miles away. A finely detailed plan involved 11 Victor tankers refuelling each other to give the Vulcan enough fuel to make its attack run. On its homeward journey the aircraft would also require refuelling before it could reach Ascension.

As it neared the Falklands the pilot took the bomber to low level to avoid radar detection before pulling up to 10,000 ft for its bombing run. The bombs were released and the Vulcan turned for home without being fired on. Reconnaissance photographs later showed a line of bomb craters, the last of which was in the middle of the runway. XM607 eventually reached Ascension, following its record-breaking mission of 15 hours and 45 minutes. Withers was awarded the Distinguished Flying Cross and his crew were mentioned in dispatches. Due to factors such as the aircraft burning more fuel than envisaged, the last accompanying Victor flew on further than planned, depleting its own reserves in order to provide the Vulcan with enough fuel. For his own actions the Victor captain, Squadron Leader Bob Tuxford, was awarded the Air Force Cross.

As well as two other Black Buck bombing raids by Vulcans there were other long-range missions from Ascension during the campaign:

► A 14-hour, 45-minute maritime radar reconnaissance flight to South Georgia flown by a Victor.

► Fleet protection sorties, flown by Nimrods.

► Anti-radar missions targeting Argentinian radar near Port Stanley, flown by Vulcans armed with Shrike missiles.

► 40 sorties in which Hercules transporters dropped supplies to the task force at sea.

WHEN THINGS DON'T GO RIGHT: VULCAN TO BRAZIL

On 3 June Vulcan XM597 had carried out a long-range anti-radar attack on Argentinian installations on the Falklands. As it took on fuel during its final air-to-air refuelling the Vulcan's probe broke off, leaving the crew with few options. They did not have enough fuel to reach Ascension and the only airfield where a landing was possible was in Brazil. The pilot, Squadron Leader Neil McDougall, used all his years of experience to bring the bomber to a safe landing, with fuel levels so low it would not have been able to complete a missed approach. The aircraft was held by Brazilian authorities and took no further part in the war. It is now on display at the National Museum of Flight in East Lothian.

Harriers

As Sea Harriers were lost to accidents and enemy action, air force Harriers were sent out to the task force. Some GR.3s were transported by ship while others were flown direct to the carriers from Ascension. These Harriers were modified for carrier use and were fitted with Sidewinder air-to-air missiles. Like many of the other modifications made during the war, they were made at high speed with great effort by the technical personnel of the air force and the civilian manufacturers. Three Harrier GR.3s were lost in combat sorties attacking Argentinian targets.

GREAT AIRCRAFT: HAWKER SIDDELEY HARRIER

Maximum speed: 730 mph
Maximum altitude: 51,000 ft

Armament:	5,000 lb payload: 2 x 1,000 lb freefall bombs, 2 x SNEB rocket pods, laser-guided bombs, 2 x AIM-9 Sidewinders, 2 x 30 mm Aden cannon (in gun pods)
Crew:	1

The Harrier was the world's first VTOL military jet aircraft to enter service, which it did with 1(F) Sqn in 1969. The Harrier's concept of vectoring its engine's thrust allowed it to operate from areas previously denied to combat aircraft. The Harrier was the first air force aircraft to feature a head-up display, giving flight and targeting information to the pilot while looking through the front windscreen, without them having to look down into the cockpit.

Dispersed operations meant they could be flown from inside forests, which made them more difficult to attack and brought them closer to the front line.

The Harrier II version featured a redesigned fuselage, more advanced avionics and a larger wing able to carry more stores. The ultimate version in British service, the GR.9A, was withdrawn from UK service in 2010 following the Strategic Defence and Security Review.

*GR.3 version.

DID YOU KNOW?

In May 1969 a Harrier achieved the fastest time in the Transatlantic Air Race by flying from London to New York in 6 hours and 11 minutes. Despite being subsonic, the Harrier's ability to take off and land in the city centre helped it win first place.

1435 Flight

Following the victory on 14 June, the air force established a permanent base at Mount Pleasant, which has been guarded since then by F-4 Phantoms, Tornado F.3s and now Typhoons, operating as 1435 Flight – a unit whose history dates back to Malta and the Second World War.

'Bravo November'

Four Chinook heavy-lift helicopters were sent to the Falklands on board the *Atlantic Conveyor* container ship. When this was sunk by Argentinian Exocet missiles, only one survived, having been flown off before the attack. ZA718, known as Bravo November after its 'BN' tail-code, was then forced to carry out the heavy lifting on its own, amounting to 1,500 troops (including 81 in one lift – twice the normal capacity) and 550 tons of supplies being carried during the remainder of the war. Showing the ruggedness of this helicopter, Bravo November survived being flown (temporarily) into the sea. It continues in service to this day.

GULF WAR 1991

In August 1990 Iraq invaded Kuwait. There was an immediate international response, with troops and aircraft being deployed to prevent further incursion into Saudi Arabia. As Coalition forces built up, a deadline for Iraqi withdrawal was issued: 15 January 1991. When this date passed without any sign of Saddam Hussein adhering to it, Coalition air forces began an intensive bombing campaign. They had overwhelming superiority, with a five-to-one advantage in numbers, as well as being technologically more advanced.

The RAF's participation was given the code name Operation Granby, and aircraft were based in Saudi Arabia, Bahrain and Oman. A large range of types took part:

► Tornado GR.1

► Tornado GR.1A

- Tornado F.3

- Buccaneer

- Jaguar

- VC10

- Victor

- Hercules

- TriStar

- Nimrod

- Chinook

- Puma.

Tornadoes were tasked with airfield attacks and suppression of enemy air defences (SEAD) sorties flown at low level before switching to medium level. The GR.1A reconnaissance version took part in the search for deployed Scud surface-to-surface missiles. In August 1990, the Tornado F.3 air defence version had been the first air force aircraft deployed to the Gulf. Jaguars targeted shipping, missile sites and artillery batteries using CRV-7 rockets and CBU-87 cluster bombs. Buccaneers were initially employed to designate targets for Tornadoes but were also used to self-designate bombing missions. The transporters carried 26,000 personnel and 54,000 tons of cargo.

Over 7,000 air force personnel were sent to the Gulf, supporting the mounting of over 6,000 operational sorties (the second highest, behind the United States).

Ground operations began on 24 February and the invasion lasted 100 hours until 28 February, when a ceasefire was declared. Five Tornado aircrew were killed in the war.

AFGHANISTAN

British aircraft supported the war in Afghanistan from October 2001. British troops were supported by Chinook helicopters, which carried combat troops, delivered supplies to army forward operating bases, and evacuated casualties. Close air support was provided by Harriers and Tornadoes, and air force intelligence, surveillance, target acquisition and reconnaissance (ISTAR) missions were flown by Sentinels. In September 2006, 14 British air force, army and marines personnel were killed when a Nimrod exploded while carrying out a reconnaissance sortie over Helmand Province. The accident, caused by a fire following in-flight refuelling, was the largest loss of military personnel in one incident since the Falklands conflict.

British combat operations in Afghanistan ended in 2014, but armed forces personnel and a small number of Chinook and then Puma helicopters remained behind to train Afghan security forces as part of Operation Toral.

IRAQ

Following the Gulf War of 1991, coalition aircraft had carried out missions enforcing a no-fly zone over the north and south of Iraq. In 1998, as the situation escalated with Saddam Hussein resisting UN inspectors looking for weapons of mass destruction (WMDs), attacks were made against targets by Tornadoes as part of Operation Desert Fox.

This containment policy was replaced by direct intervention in March 2003 when a US-led force invaded in order to remove Saddam Hussein from power. British forces in Operation Telic were the second largest after those of the United States. The initial stage of combat operations ended after a short campaign although an insurgency led to continuing military operations. The RAF contribution amounted to over 100 fixed-wing aircraft that flew more than 2,500 missions. Smart weapons made up the majority of munitions used. Combat operations under Telic ended in 2009 with all of the United Kingdom's forces being withdrawn in 2011.

LIBYA

In 2011, as part of Operation Ellamy the air force flew missions to protect the Libyan civilian population during the country's civil war. It also evacuated UK nationals from the country.

Tornadoes began by flying directly from Marham to Libya and then returning after using the Storm Shadow stand-off missile. This 3,000-mile mission was supported by air-refuelling VC10 and TriStar tankers, while Sentinel and E-3D Sentry aircraft also took part. Ellamy saw the combat introduction of the Eurofighter Typhoon in the ground attack role.

Over 3,000 sorties had been flown when the operation ended in October.

SYRIA AND IRAQ

In September 2014 the Iraqi government requested assistance to counter the threat of ISIS. The air force had been carrying out humanitarian aid in the north of the country since August but the role was expanded in the face of ISIS action. Rivet Joint was introduced for the first time and Tornadoes carried out air strikes.

British aircraft were not permitted to carry out combat actions in Syria but this changed in December 2015. Tornadoes and Typhoons assigned to these missions flew from Cyprus. Reaper UAVs were also utilised for surveillance and attack, using laser-guided GBU-12 bombs and Hellfire missiles.

THE RAF TODAY

Structure

Over the past 100 years the RAF has undergone several changes in its organisational structure, with different commands serving different functions, leading up to the current situation with Air Command, formed on 1 April 2007 when Personnel & Training and Strike Command merged. (Strike Command was the result of a previous amalgamation of Fighter, Bomber and Transport Commands).

Within Air Command there are four groups:

1 Group	Combat aircraft, ISTAR
2 Group	Air combat support (transport aircraft, aerial tankers, force protection)
22 (Training) Group	Recruitment and training of personnel
38 Group	Logistics, engineering, communications and medical.

Current airfields

Many of the most famous airfields are no longer operated by the air force: Biggin Hill is a civilian airfield, Duxford is home to part of the Imperial War Museums and Leuchars is an army base. Some other famous names from the air force's past such as Henlow and Halton face eventual closure. However, many stations with a long record of operations remain in service. They include:

Base	Location	Details
Akrotiri	Cyprus	Staging base, home to 84 Sqn's Griffins and used by Red Arrows for winter training
Ascension Island	South Atlantic	Staging base for flights to and from the Falkland Islands
Benson	Oxfordshire	Support helicopter base
Boulmer	Northumberland	Non-flying station, home to the School of Aerospace Battle Management and the Aerospace Surveillance and Control Systems HQ

Brize Norton	Oxfordshire	Air force's air transport centre
Coningsby	Lincolnshire	Fighter base for Typhoons and the Battle of Britain Memorial Flight
Cosford	Shropshire	Defence School of Aeronautical Engineering
Cranwell	Lincolnshire	Home of the RAF College and HQ of Air Cadets
Gibraltar	Iberian Peninsula	Staging base for operations in the Mediterranean
Halton	Buckinghamshire	Training base for initial non-commissioned recruit training and further development training
Henlow	Bedfordshire	Amongst the various units is the RAF Centre for Aviation Medicine
High Wycombe	Buckinghamshire	HQ to Air Command
Honington	Suffolk	HQ to RAF Regiment
Leeming	North Yorkshire	Home to 100 Sqn as well as various other units
Linton-on-Ouse	North Yorkshire	Basic fast-jet pilot training
Lossiemouth	Moray	Typhoon and Tornado squadrons
Marham	Norfolk	Main Tornado base, soon to be the first F-35 station
Mount Pleasant	Falkland Islands	Home to transport facilities and 1435 Flight fighter defence
Northolt	London	Only remaining operational Battle of Britain flying station; home to 32 Sqn
Odiham	Hampshire	Helicopter base with Chinooks
Scampton	Lincolnshire	Base of the Red Arrows

Shawbury	Shropshire	Helicopter training base, and home to the Defence Helicopter Flying School, the Central Flying School (Helicopter) Sqn and the School of Air Operations Control
Valley	Anglesey	Advanced fast-jet training base, with Hawk T.2 and helicopter training with Griffin
Waddington	Lincolnshire	Former V-bomber base, now home of ISTAR aircraft
Wittering	Cambridgeshire	Elementary flying training with No. 3 Flying Training School, and University Air Squadrons (UAS) and Air Cadets' Air Experience Flights (AEF) flying supervised by No. 6 Flying Training School
Wyton	Cambridgeshire	Joint Forces Command station with various units including Headquarters Joint Forces Intelligence Group (JFIG)

'El Adem with grass'

NICKNAME GIVEN TO MARHAM IN NORFOLK, DUE TO THE SIMILARITY OF ITS FLAT, FEATURELESS TERRAIN TO THAT OF THE BASE IN LIBYA

Present-day acronyms

ACSSU	Air Combat Service Support Unit
ASACS	Aerospace Surveillance and Control System
CMRS	Capability-based Module Readiness System
DGIFC	Defence Geospatial Intelligence Fusion Centre

DSCIS	Defence School of Communications and Information Systems
FOAV	Formal Operational Assurance Visit
JFACTSU	Joint Forward Air Controller Training and Standards Unit
MEATU	Multi-Engine Aircrew Training Unit
UKMFTS	United Kingdom Military Flying Training System
SEARW	Single Engine Advanced Rotary Wing

PART 2

THE ARMS

CHAPTER FIVE

TRADES AND BRANCHES

The air force has organised its personnel into trades and branches based on the specialisms required. Some have changed over the years but the general principles remain.

NON-COMMISSIONED TRADES

Like the navy but unlike the army, the RAF has always been a technology-focused organisation, operating machines for a military purpose. In order to operate them effectively the service requires personnel with the appropriate skills and experience.

When the RFC was formed in 1912 the need for skilled men (to be aged between 18 and 30 and no smaller than 5 ft 2 in) was outlined. It was primarily looking for those who had been apprenticed in a mechanical engineer's workshop and had also worked in a motor engineering works. Those who had experience as an aeroplane mechanic were also welcomed. Men who had been employed in other trades (not all of which were needed to work directly with the aircraft) were also required:

blacksmiths
carpenters
clerks
coppersmiths
draughtsmen
electricians
fitters
harness makers
instrument repairers
joiners

metal turners
painters
photographers
riggers
sailmakers
tinsmiths
wheelwrights
whitesmiths
wireless operators
wood turners

Those in the following minor trades were also required:

cable jointers
chauffeurs
drillers
dynamo attendants
electric bell fitters
joiners' helpers

machinists
motor fitters
plumbers' mates
switchboard attendants
tool grinders
wiremen

DID YOU KNOW?

Fighter ace James McCudden was a mechanic before becoming a pilot in the RFC. A similar route through the ranks to that of commissioned aircrew would be followed by many more throughout the following decades.

In the decades after the war the pace of aircraft development was not as rapid as during wartime, but the changes that did come into effect were reflected in the type of trades needed. Chief amongst them was the use of metal as the main material for aircraft construction, instead of wood, although machines

like the Hurricane and Wellington were still partially covered in fabric and so the skills used in doping and painting the material were still required during the Second World War.

That war resulted in a huge expansion of personnel in uniform. For non-commissioned ground crew, the trades available for new recruits in 1941 were placed in six groups. They were arranged in order of highest pay first, reflecting the different skills required, with Group I earning from 3/9 to 16/6 a day and those in the lower-skilled Group M on 2/- to 13/6 a day. Additional pay could be given for working during wartime, having certain qualifications and exhibiting good conduct.

Group I
Blacksmith and welder
Coppersmith and sheet metalworker
Draughtsman
Electrician
Engine driver
Fitter (airframe)
Fitter (armourer)
Fitter (engine)
Fitter (marine)
Fitter (motor transport)
Fitter (torpedo)
Instrument maker
Instrument repairer
Link trainer instructor
Machine tool setter and operator
Metalworker
Radio mechanic
Wireless mechanic
Wireless operator mechanic

Group II
Acetylene welder
Armoured car crew
Armourer
Balloon operator
Blacksmith
Carpenter
Coppersmith
Electrician
Flight mechanic
Grinder
Instrument repairer
Meteorologist
Miller
MT mechanic
Photographer

Radio operator
Sheet metalworker
Turner
Wireless operator

Group III
Balloon rigger
Balloon fabric worker
Balloon winch driver
Cook and butcher
Fabric worker
Hydrogen worker
Motorboat crew
Parachute repairer
Shoemaker
Tailor

Group IV
Clerk (accounting)
Clerk (general duties)
Clerk (pay accounting)
Clerk (special duties)
Equipment assistant
Radiotelephony operator
Teleprinter operator

Group V
Aircrafthand
Barber
Batman

Driver (MT)
Ground gunner
Machine-gun instructor
Messing duties
Motorcyclist
Musician
Parachute packer
Physical training instructor
Pigeon keeper
Service police
Telephone operator
Torpedoman

Group M
Dental clerk orderly
Dental mechanic
Dental orderly (under training)
Dispenser
Laboratory assistant
Masseur
Medical orderly (under training)
Mental nursing orderly
Nursing orderly
Operating room assistant
Radiographer
Sanitary assistant
Special treatment orderly
Trained nurse

DID YOU KNOW?

On the night of 27 February 1942, radar technician Flight Sergeant Charles Cox played a vital part in an unusual raid. A German Würzburg radar site had been spotted at Bruneval on the north coast of France. Cox, who had never flown let alone parachuted before, was dropped with army paratroops near to the site. Despite coming under fire, Cox was able to retrieve key parts of the radar and bring them back for analysis. He was awarded the Military Medal.

After the Second World War the RAF experienced a reduction in numbers, from over a million in 1945 to a fifth of that by 1950. The reduction in personnel put a strain on the service with a lack of skilled men. Conscription through national service brought in some of those with the skills required, but they were only in for a limited time, their effective period of service being shorter than for regulars.

Up until 1951 around a hundred trades were organised into four bands – A, B, C and D – corresponding to differing levels of pay. That year saw a new trade structure comprising 22 trade groups; within each specialisation were different grades, to allow advancement within that trade rather than as it had been previously, where an airman had to remuster if they wanted to progress. Levels in each of the new trade groups went from unskilled up to advanced. Two means of promotion were also introduced, through a command stream and a technician stream. This created new ranks, such as Chief Technician and Senior Technician.

BRANCHES

In the RFC, initially all the officers were pilots, but during the war some could be assigned to staff positions or become equipment officers. After the war, Trenchard believed that all officers in the service should be pilots except for those in branches such as accounts, stores/equipment, medical, dental, legal and chaplains.

Up to 1939 all pilots entered the general duties branch, where they would learn to fly first and could then specialise in technical areas, but after this year officers could enter directly into the technical branch, which contained engineering, armaments and signals.

As the service expanded and developed during the war, there were other changes and by 1959 the five main branches were:

- General duties (flying and executive)
- Technical (later to become engineering)
- Secretarial (including accounts)
- Equipment
- RAF Regiment.

Others were:

- Provost (RAF police)
- Catering
- Marine
- Physical fitness
- Airfield construction
- Education
- Legal
- Chaplains
- Medical
- Dental.

In terms of promotion, those in the specialised branches were not able to rise beyond the head of their branch, while senior officers would only come from the general duties branch. Further changes made to the branch structure of the air force are reflected in the current roles available in the service:

Technical and engineering
Aircraft Technician (avionics)
Aircraft Technician (mechanical)
Communications Infrastructure Technician
Cyberspace Communication Specialist (formerly ICT Technician)
Electrician
Engineer Officer (aerosystems)
Engineer Officer (communications electronics)
General Technician Workshop
Survival Equipment Specialist
Vehicle and Mechanical Equipment Technician
Weapon Technician

Air operations support
Aerospace Battle Managers
Aerospace Systems Operator
Air Cartographer
Air Traffic Control Officer
Air Traffic Controller (Senior NCO)
Flight Operations Assistant
Flight Operations Manager
Flight Operations Officer

Medical
Biomedical Scientist
Dental Nurse
Dental Officer
Environmental Health Technician
Medical Officer (doctor)

Medical Support Officer
Medical Support Officer (physio)
Nursing Officer
Operating Department Practitioner
Paramedic
Pharmacy Technician
Radiographer
RAF Medic
Registered Nurse (adult)
Registered Nurse (mental health)
Student Nurse (adult)

Personnel support
Chaplain
Human Resources
Musician
Personnel Support Officer
Personnel Training Officer
Physical Training Instructor
Legal Officer
Media Operations Officer

Logistics
Catering and Hospitality Specialist
Chef
Driver
Logistics Officer
Mover
Supply, Storage and Distribution Specialist

Force protection
Firefighter
RAF Police
RAF Police Officer
RAF Regiment Gunner

RAF Regiment Officer

Intelligence
Intelligence Analyst
Intelligence Analyst (linguist)
Intelligence Officer
Joint Cyber Unit
Photographer

Aircrew
Pilot
Pilot (remotely piloted aircraft system)
Weapons Systems Officer
Weapons Systems Operator
Weapons Systems Operator (linguist)

NICKNAMES
The RAF is fond of using nicknames as shorthand. Some of those connected with specific roles include:

Liney	Flight Line Mechanic
Loadey	Air Loadmaster
Shinee	Air Traffic Control
Sooty	Engine Mechanic
Staish	Station Commander
Wobbly	Warrant Officer
Squinto	Squadron Intelligence Officer
Penguin	Ex-aircrew now on ground duties
Rock ape	RAF Regiment
Snowdrop	RAF Police
Dumpie	Bomb Dump Technician
Gripper	Ground Equipper

WHEN THINGS DON'T GO RIGHT: LIGHTNING FLIGHT

In July 1966 one engineering officer achieved a unique place in the history of the service. Wing Commander 'Taffy' Holden was based at RAF Lyneham and working on Lightnings. He was in the cockpit carrying out ground runs when he inadvertently pushed the two engines into reheat. The powerful jet fighter quickly took to the air and Holden, who was a qualified light aircraft pilot, was forced to fly his new type. He was unable to eject as the seat was not live and so he continued to fly circuits until confident enough to attempt a landing, which he successfully carried out.

MEDICAL BRANCH

'The duties of a medical officer in the Air Force included not only the prevention and treatment of those ordinary diseases to which the personnel of any fighting service are liable, but the special study of the mental and physical stresses imposed on the airman in diverse circumstances and climates – a new branch of medicine which still provided considerable scope for research.'

THE LANCET, 28 AUGUST 1926

The medical branch has been in existence since the service's very beginnings, with the Royal Air Force Medical Services (RAFMS) being established in 1918. The Second World War saw the advent of aeromedical evacuation and by the end of that conflict almost half a million service personnel had been transported, with

200,000 of them in Burma where the difficult terrain made ground transportation of casualties almost impossible.

In the present day the branch consists of regular and reserve personnel. Its role is to ensure all air force personnel in the UK and those deployed overseas are given adequate healthcare. The RAFMS's tactical medical wing (TMW) organises deployed medical treatment facilities in theatre, provided by deployable aeromedical response teams (DARTS) which are kept on six-hour notice. The TMW is responsible for aeromedical evacuations of injured or sick personnel from overseas back to the UK, using critical care air support teams (CCAST), which provide airborne intensive care.

Another part of the RAFMS is the Centre for Aviation Medicine (CAM) at Henlow, which is the main organisation for research into aviation medicine in the UK and uses two Hawk T.1 aircraft based at Boscombe Down. One part of CAM's work is training air force aircrew in the effects of hypoxia (oxygen deficiency) using hyperbaric chambers.

Princess Mary's Royal Air Force Nursing Service

In June 1918 the RAF Nursing Service was established. It had previously been provided by the Royal Army Medical Corps and the Voluntary Aid Detachment. In 1923 the nursing service was named Princess Mary's Royal Air Force Nursing Service (PMRAFNS). In 1943 nursing officers were given equivalent air force ranks:

Matron-in-chief	Air Commodore
Chief principal matron	Group Captain
Principal matron	Wing Commander
Matron	Squadron Leader
Senior sister	Flight Lieutenant
Sister	Flying Officer

The PMRAFNS continues to be the nursing branch of the RAF. In 1980 it changed from being women only.

RAF REGIMENT

> *'It's better to start the war with 800 bombers*
> *operating from reasonably secure bases than with*
> *1,000 bombers, of whom perhaps more than half will*
> *be unable to operate because their aerodromes have*
> *been put out of action.'*

**GROUP CAPTAIN JOHN SLESSOR, DEPUTY DIRECTOR OF PLANS,
AIR MINISTRY, IN A LETTER TO THE DEPUTY CHIEF OF AIR
STAFF, 1938**

In the 1920s RAF personnel had carried out combat roles with the armoured car companies and levy forces in the Middle East. In the lead up to the Second World War the air force had little provision for UK airfield defence as the army was unable to provide sufficient resources. Ground gunners were recruited and by October 1940 they numbered 35,000. They were armed with light machine guns and heavier weapons such as the 40 mm Bofors gun. In the Battle of Britain, Corporal Bruce Jackman was awarded the first Military Medal ever given to a ground gunner, for taking over a Lewis gun position at Detling while under enemy attack and continuing to fire until the post was destroyed. He was seriously injured during the action.

The invasion of Crete in May 1941 brought home the vulnerability of airfields to airborne forces and inspired the formation of the RAF Regiment the following year. This was given responsibility to defend RAF installations in the UK, but Regiment squadrons also took part in the Desert War, the invasion of North Africa and the advance through north-west Europe following the D-Day landings. During these campaigns they were also used as an offensive force. In the Far East, Regiment troops helped produce victory in securing the vital Meiktila airfield in Burma against continuous Japanese attacks.

By the end of the war the Regiment's 85,000 personnel were spread across 74 squadrons in northern Europe, 24 in the Mediterranean and 33 in the Far East. But, as with the rest of the RAF, the Regiment experienced a massive reduction in size following the end of the war, ending up with 29 squadrons.

Post-war, Regiment personnel served in Malaya, Singapore, Aden, Belize, Cyprus, Northern Ireland, Kuwait, Iraq, Kosovo and Afghanistan amongst other locations where RAF assets were based. There was particular concern about Soviet special forces being used to attack airfields in Germany and the UK, and the Regiment were trained to repel such attacks.

From 1947, regular Regiment units were supplemented by those of the Royal Auxiliary Air Force Regiment, although these were disbanded following the 1957 Defence White Paper. Re-formed in 1979, it is currently constituted of six auxiliary Regiment squadrons and one flight.

In 2004 the responsibility of operating the short-range Rapier defence missile batteries was taken over by the army's Royal Artillery, albeit under RAF command.

DID YOU KNOW?

Members of the Regiment work with the Special Air Service, Special Boat Service and Special Reconnaissance Regiment as part of the Special Forces Support Group.

QUEEN'S COLOUR SQN

The Queen's Colour Sqn has a dual role: performing ceremonial duties and as a field squadron in its guise of 63 Sqn RAF Regiment. It represents the RAF on formal occasions such as the Remembrance Day commemoration at the Cenotaph in London and the State Opening of Parliament, and in public events such as the Royal

Edinburgh Military Tattoo. The squadron is the official escort of the RAF's Queen's Colour.

RAF POLICE

The world's oldest air force police service was formed on 1 April 1918. Presently part of Force Protection, it provides a range of policing tasks similar to that of the civilian police. The head of the police is the Provost Marshal. During the Second World War police brought to justice many of those Nazis involved in the mass execution of the aircrew who took part in 'The Great Escape'.

One of the features of the police service is its dogs, which were introduced in 1944 as guard dogs. Owners volunteered their pets for wartime service which were then given back after the war's end.

Air dogs are trained primarily in airfield security and also in searching for drugs and explosives. An arms and explosive search dog is the equivalent of a nine-person search team. The RAF's police is the only one of the British armed forces to use military working dogs.

DID YOU KNOW?

Policemen and women are distinguished by their white-topped caps, giving rise to the nickname 'Snowdrops'.

CHAPLAINS BRANCH

This branch has provided religious teaching and pastoral care to servicemen and women since the very start of the service in 1918. The first chaplain-in-chief was the Reverend Harry Viener, who was seconded from the navy. By the end of the war the chaplaincy service had 60 chaplains. But, as with the personnel and aircraft, this saw a large reduction and by 1919 they numbered 29.

As outlined in the Queen's Regulations, chaplains hold relative rank 'solely for the purposes of defining status as regards precedence, discipline and administration'. The chaplain-in-chief is the same level as an air vice-marshal.

Chaplains are from Christian churches but there is provision for other faiths, provided by chaplains who operate across the other armed forces. They are attached to units at home and abroad.

CHAPTER SIX

SQUADRONS

Squadrons are the air force's essential operational unit. The format originated in the RFC and has remained much the same ever since. In the 1930s each squadron's badge and motto were approved by the Inspector of RAF Badges. Previous to this, units had come up with their own. For instance, 72 Sqn decided on a shield, which included a pint tankard, a crashed aircraft and the motto 'Altera Potatio non Nocebit' (Another drink won't do us any harm). Needless to say this was not approved and the current badge depicts a swift.

CURRENT FRONT-LINE SQUADRONS

While the number of current squadrons is much less than in previous years, some famous numbers still form part of the RAF's collective strength.

1 (Fighter) Squadron

Motto:	'First in all things'
Badge:	Numeral 'I' surrounded by wings
Current aircraft:	Typhoon

The world's oldest operational flying unit was formed in April 1912. It saw action in the First World War flying the Nieuport 17 and SE.5a. In the interwar period it took part in the air policing of India and Iraq before returning to the UK where it was equipped with Hawker Furies. Hurricanes, 1(F) Sqn flew first in France then the Battle of Britain, and was a night fighter unit in the Blitz before receiving Hawker Typhoon ground attack aircraft. It then flew Spitfires on cross-Channel 'Rhubarb' missions – low-level sorties to find targets of opportunity – and later defended the UK against V1 flying bombs. Its post-war jets were the Meteor, the Hunter and the Harrier, which it operated in the Falklands conflict. In 2012 it received the Typhoon, with which it is now based at Lossiemouth.

RAF TRADITIONS

Timing

1(F) Sqn start their formal squadron dinners at 19.45 as those numerals had a certain historical significance.

II (Army Cooperation) Squadron

Motto: 'Hereward'
Badge: Rope 'Wake knot' over a roundel
Current aircraft: Typhoon

Known as the 'Shiny Two', the unit formed with a mixture of types in 1912 and was the first to deploy to France in 1914. The knot used in the badge symbolised the ties with the army as it operated in the army cooperation role. In the Second World War it flew Lysanders, Mustangs and Spitfires, and after the war continued the reconnaissance role in Germany with Meteors, Swifts, Hunters, Phantoms, Jaguars and Tornadoes. It began operating the Typhoon in 2015.

3 (Fighter) Squadron

Motto: 'The third shall be first'
Badge: A cockatrice standing on a monolith
Current aircraft: Typhoon

3 Sqn's motto stems from its establishment as the first complete squadron to be formed in the RFC in May 1912. It carried out various roles in the First World War and in the interwar period before taking its Hurricanes to France in 1940. It used Tempests against V1s and after moving to Germany remained there post-war, flying a mixture of jets before being equipped with the Harrier in 1972, which it operated until 2006. It was the first UK front-line unit to be equipped with the Typhoon. In 2012, 3 Sqn Typhoons were the first fighters to be stationed in London since the Second World War, as air defenders for the Olympic Games.

V (Army Cooperation) Squadron

Motto: 'Thou mayst break, but shall not bend me'
Badge: A maple leaf
Current aircraft: Sentinel

V (or 5) Sqn began at Farnborough in 1913 and flew artillery-spotting missions over the Western Front. Along the North-West Frontier it operated Westland Wapitis, which were kept until the Second World War when the squadron was equipped with another biplane, the Hawker Hart. It then flew Hawker Audaxes, Curtiss Mohawks, Hurricanes and P-47 Thunderbolts in India during the Burma Campaign. As with many of its counterparts it was stationed in Germany post-war, until in 1965 it moved to Binbrook with the Lightning. 5 Sqn continued in the air defence role with Tornado

F.3s at Coningsby before disbanding in 2003. It re-formed with the Sentinel, with which it continues its army cooperation tasks.

6 Squadron

Motto: 'The eyes of the army'
Badge: An eagle attacking a serpent
Current aircraft: Typhoon

The 'Flying Tin Openers' (later 'Can Openers') gained their nickname during the Second World War with their Hurricanes' ability to destroy German tanks during the Desert War. The squadron had begun its operational life during the First World War where in 1915 one of its pilots, Captain Lanoe Hawker, was the first aerial recipient of the Victoria Cross. After the Second World War the unit was based in the Middle East and while in Jordan received a personal standard from the Jordanian king. It is the only air force squadron with two standards. It returned to the UK in 1969 for the first time in 50 years to receive Phantoms but replaced these with Jaguars five years later, which it was still operating in the First Gulf War in 1990–91. It received the Typhoon in 2010, and in 2014 a special 100th anniversary paint scheme was applied in the colours of its Desert War predecessors.

7 Squadron

Motto: 'By day and by night'
Badge: Constellation of Ursa Major
Current aircraft: Chinook

Like other early squadrons 7 Sqn flew army support missions over the Western Front. In 1923 it took on the heavy night bomber role, which it kept until the start of the Second World War by which time it was training Hampden crews. In 1940 it was the first squadron to operate the Short Stirling, the first of the British four-engine heavy bombers. Post-war, Lincolns were used in Malaya before the squadron received Valiants when it became a V-bomber unit. Following a period flying the Canberra, in 1982 7 Sqn changed roles and began operating the Chinook helicopter.

8 Squadron

Motto:	'Everywhere unbounded'
Badge:	An Arabian dagger
Current aircraft:	E-3 Sentry

8 Sqn has spent most of its operational life overseas: in Egypt, Iraq, East Africa, Ceylon and Aden, where it flew the Hunter in ground-attack sorties. In 1972 it began flying the Avro Shackleton in the airborne early warning (AEW) role; it has continued with the E-3 Sentry since 1991.

DID YOU KNOW?

Avro Shackletons of 8 Sqn were named after characters in the children's TV show *The Magic Roundabout*: PC Knapweed, Sage, Florence, Paul, Mr Rusty, Brian, Mr McHenry, Ermintrude, Rosalie, Dougal, Parsley and Dill.

IX (Bomber) Squadron

Motto:	'Through the night we fly'
Badge:	A bat
Current aircraft:	Tornado

Formed as the first RFC unit equipped with radio for the artillery spotting role, 9 Sqn trained other units in its use. It then was a night-bomber squadron flying the Vickers Vimy, Virginia and Handley Page Heyford before receiving Wellingtons in time for the Second World War, when it flew the first bombing mission of the war. Lancasters of

9 Sqn helped capsize the *Tirpitz* in 1944. Post-war it was a V-bomber Vulcan unit, and in January 1982 it became the first operational RAF squadron to receive the Panavia Tornado.

DID YOU KNOW?

At Honington the hardened aircraft shelter site for IX (B) Sqn was known as Gotham City.

10 Squadron

Motto:	'To hit the mark'
Badge:	A winged arrow
Current aircraft:	Voyager

Now a transport/tanker unit, 10 Sqn began in the reconnaissance role in France in 1915. Between the wars it flew heavy bombers such as the Hyderabad, Hinaidi, Virginia and Heyford. With Whitleys 10 Sqn was the first RAF squadron to overfly Berlin in October 1939. As a transport unit it took part in the Berlin Airlift and after a period as a bomber squadron with Canberras and Victors, it received the Vickers VC10 airliner in 1966 (and then the aerial tanker version from 1992), which it operated until 2005. In 2011 10 Sqn re-formed with the Voyager.

XI (Fighter) Squadron

Motto:	'Swifter and keener than eagles'
Badge:	Two eagles flying together
Current aircraft:	Typhoon

11 Sqn holds the honour of having been the world's first pure fighter squadron when it was formed on 14 February 1915. It operated in the

air-policing role before, during the Second World War, its Blenheims flew bombing missions in Africa, Greece then South East Asia. Jets were received in 1950, beginning with the Vampire and then the Venom. Later, the squadron was equipped with Lightnings, which were in turn replaced by the Tornado F.3 in 1988.

12 (Bomber) Squadron

Motto:	'Leads the field'
Badge:	A fox mask
Current aircraft:	Tornado

12 Sqn was formed on 14 February 1915 from a nucleus of personnel from 1 Sqn. Originally engaged in reconnaissance it carried out bombing and ground attack missions on the Western Front. In the Second World War it suffered heavy losses in France in 1940 flying the Fairey Battle; two Victoria Crosses were awarded following one attack. After the war its Canberras flew during the Suez Campaign and it formed part of the V-bomber force with the Vulcan. In 1969 it was equipped with the Blackburn Buccaneer for the maritime attack role at Lossiemouth before these were exchanged for the Tornado in 1993.

DID YOU KNOW?

In 1925 the Fairey Fox was introduced. 12 Sqn were its only operators, as a result of which they adopted the animal for their unit badge.

13 Squadron

Motto:	'We assist by watching'
Badge:	A lynx's head in front of a dagger
Current aircraft:	Reaper

13 Sqn's operations in the First World War were notable for the first formation bombing raid in November 1916. After the war the squadron flew a range of aircraft until in 1940 it was equipped with Lysanders in France but, similar to other units facing the Blitzkrieg, was forced to withdraw across the Channel. It took part in the Dieppe raid in 1942, its Blenheims laying smokescreens. After the war it was employed in the reconnaissance role, with Canberras then Tornado GR.1As, before in 2012 it became the first UK-based operator of the Reaper RPAS (remotely piloted air system).

14 Squadron

Motto:	'I spread my wings and keep my promise'
Badge:	A winged plate charged with a cross throughout and shoulder pieces of a suit of armour
Current aircraft:	Shadow

14 Sqn spent its first three decades in the Middle East until in 1944 it returned to the UK. Post-war it was again overseas, being stationed in Germany operating Mosquitoes, Vampires, Venoms, Canberras, Phantoms, Jaguars and latterly the Tornado. In 2011 it began operating the Shadow R.1 reconnaissance aircraft from Waddington.

18 Squadron

Motto:	'With courage and faith'
Badge:	A pegasus
Current aircraft:	Chinook

18 Sqn flew FE.2bs in tactical reconnaissance sorties at the Battle of the Somme, and in the Second World War Blenheims were used against barges in the Channel ports, shipping in the Mediterranean and German bases in Tunisia. 18 Sqn's Dakotas took part in the Berlin Airlift before it regained its status as a bomber unit with Canberras and then Valiants. It began its current role as a helicopter squadron in 1964 with the Wessex.

27 Squadron

Motto: 'With all speed to the stars'
Badge: An elephant
Current aircraft: Chinook

27 Sqn's use of the Martinsyde G.100 Elephant during the First World War provided inspiration for its unit badge. The squadron has carried out a wide variety of roles – fighter escort, bomber, reconnaissance, air policing, maritime strike, jungle supply, cargo transport, glider towing, paratrooper dropping, nuclear strike and maritime reconnaissance – before becoming a helicopter operational conversion unit. It now operates the Chinook in the support helicopter role.

30 Squadron

Motto: 'All out'
Badge: A palm tree
Current aircraft: Hercules

Appropriately for a transport squadron, 30 Sqn carried out the first aerial supply missions in 1916 at Kut-al-Amara. It operated in the Desert War until in 1941 it was sent to Crete, where it suffered heavy losses. In 1942 30 Sqn's Hurricanes were embarked on HMS *Indomitable* to Ceylon to defend Colombo, and the squadron ended the war flying P-47 Thunderbolts in Burma and India. It began its transport duties flying Dakotas in the Berlin Airlift and continued with Vickers Valettas and Blackburn Beverleys before receiving its current aircraft, the Lockheed C-130 Hercules, in 1968.

31 Squadron

Motto: 'First into Indian skies'
Badge: A mullet in front of a laurel wreath
Current aircraft: Tornado

The unit badge's mullet represents the Star of India, as 31 Sqn was formed in 1915 with the intention of operating in that country.

The 'Goldstar Squadron' was a transport unit until the 1950s, when it flew reconnaissance Canberras. Before the current Tornado, 31 Sqn was equipped with the Phantom and Jaguar.

32 (The Royal) Squadron

Motto: 'Rally round, comrades'
Badge: A stringed hunting horn
Current aircraft: BAe 146

Following a history of flying fighters in both world wars before operating the Canberra, in 1969 32 Sqn took over the Metropolitan Communications Squadron performing communications tasks with fixed-wing aircraft and helicopters. In 1995 the Queen's Flight was amalgamated into the squadron, which transported members of the Royal Family until 1999. Based at Northolt, it is now tasked with transporting VIPs and other personnel in BAe 146 airliners and an AgustaWestland AW109 Grand New helicopter.

33 Squadron

Motto: 'Loyalty'
Badge: A hart's head
Current aircraft: Puma

33 Sqn was a home air defence unit during the First World War. In 1930, it became the first squadron to receive the Hawker Hart bomber, which gave inspiration for the unit badge. It continued with biplanes into the Second World War, flying Gladiators in the Desert War. 33 Sqn supported the D-Day landings and as part of Second Allied Tactical Air Force (2ATAF) operated over Germany until the war ended. In 1971 it was the first RAF squadron to receive the Puma.

39 Squadron

Motto: 'By day and night'
Badge: A winged bomb
Current aircraft: Reaper

39 Sqn was a home defence unit in the First World War, defending London against Zeppelin attack, and in September 1916 Lieutenant William Leefe Robinson was awarded the Victoria Cross for downing the first airship over the UK. In 1928 the squadron left the UK and as with many of its counterparts operated in the air-policing role in India. In the Second World War it operated the Beaufort torpedo bomber in the Mediterranean. It wasn't until 1970 that it returned to the UK with its photo reconnaissance Canberras, which it operated until that classic British aircraft was retired from service in 2006. In 2007, 39 Sqn began operating the Reaper RPAS from Creech Air Force Base in Nevada, USA, with the aircraft based in theatre.

47 Squadron

Motto: 'The name of the Nile is an omen of our strength'
Badge: A crane's head in front of a fountain
Current aircraft: Hercules

47 Sqn was first based in Salonika during the First World War and then in 1919 operated against communist forces in Russia. In 1946 it became a transportation unit flying the Halifax; in 1948 it was the first RAF squadron to be equipped with the Hastings; and in 1956 it was first to fly the Beverley. It began its association with the Hercules in 1968.

51 Squadron

Motto: 'Swift and sure'
Badge: A red goose
Current aircraft: RC-135W

51 Sqn was a fighter, bomber and transport unit before becoming tasked with gathering electronic intelligence (ELINT) in 1958, a role it continues to this day. On these secretive missions it flew Lincolns, Canberras and Comets before receiving the Nimrod R.1 in 1974. This was replaced by the American-built RC-135W Rivet Joint in 2013.

70 Squadron

Motto:	'Anywhere'
Badge:	A winged lion
Current aircraft:	Atlas

70 Sqn has been the first RFC or RAF unit to receive various types: the Sopwith 1 1/2 Strutter in 1916, the Sopwith Camel in 1917 and the A400M Atlas in 2015. Its newest aircraft denotes a return to the transport role it had previously carried out when in 1928 in Afghanistan it took part in the world's first airborne mass evacuation.

84 Squadron

Motto:	'Scorpions sting'
Badge:	A scorpion
Current aircraft:	Griffin

84 Sqn was formed in 1917 and served in France, then in Germany, as part of the occupation force until being disbanded in January 1920. When it re-formed later that year it moved overseas, where it has operated ever since. It currently flies the search and rescue Griffin HAR.2 in Cyprus. Since the retirement of 22 Sqn's Sea Kings in 2015, 84 Sqn is the only remaining RAF unit tasked with this role.

99 Squadron

Motto:	'Each tenacious'
Badge:	A puma
Current aircraft:	C-17

The squadron flew bombers such as the DH.9, Vimy, Heyford, Wellington and Liberator before becoming a transport unit in 1945 flying Avro Yorks. It disbanded in 1976 but after being re-formed in 2000 received the Boeing C-17 Globemaster III.

101 Squadron

Motto:	'Mind over matter'

Badge: A lion rampant in the battlements of a tower
Current aircraft: Voyager

101 Sqn flew the Sidestrand and the Overstrand in the bomber role during the 1930s, and then Blenheims, Wellingtons and Lancasters in the Second World War. The Lancasters were tasked with electronic countermeasures, using Airborne Cigar equipment to jam German communications. The squadron was disbanded in 1957 but stood up a year later as a Vulcan V-bomber unit. In 1984 it switched to the air-tanker role with the VC10 until this aircraft's retirement in 2013.

230 Squadron
Motto: 'We seek far'
Badge: A tiger in front of a palm tree
Current aircraft: Puma

230 Sqn began as a flying boat unit, operating the Felixstowe F.2A and later flew Short Singapores and Sunderlands. It spent several years as a light transport squadron before receiving its first helicopters in 1962. It has since operated Pumas in Northern Ireland, Germany and Iraq.

617 Squadron
Motto: 'After me, the flood'*
Badge: A dam being broken by three lightning flashes
Current aircraft: F-35

Perhaps the most famous squadron in the RAF, 617 Sqn was formed for one special mission: to use a 'bouncing bomb' on the Ruhr dams. It continued precision bombing raids throughout the remainder of the war and was a V-bomber unit with the Vulcan until receiving Tornadoes, which it operated until 2014. In 2016 it re-formed at the United States Marine Corps Air Station Beaufort in South Carolina, USA, to prepare for the introduction to service of the Lockheed Martin F-35.

* The Dambusters' motto was taken from a quote by Marie Antoinette, *'Après nous, le déluge'*, but it was changed to *'Après moi, le déluge'* to avoid any connection with the unfortunate French monarch.

RAF TRADITIONS

Tirpitz

Rivalry between certain squadrons, often when sharing an airfield, is a common feature of the service. One of the most well known is between the two squadrons that claim to have sunk the *Tirpitz*: 9 and 617. When a bulwark from the German warship was given to Bomber Command by the Norwegian air force it became the source of competition, and ownership was exchanged several times with the prize residing in the 'owners" mess until it was reacquired. The bulwark is now in the neutral stewardship of the RAF Museum.

DID YOU KNOW?

A broom displayed on 40 Sqn's badge comes from the First World War boast of Edward Mannock, who reasoned that the RFC could 'sweep the Hun right out of the sky'.

RESERVE, TRAINING, OPERATIONAL CONVERSION UNITS

Some of the service's notable squadron numbers have been preserved through being assigned to training units, some with a reserve capability.

No	Motto	Badge	Aircraft	Role
IV (Reserve)	'To see into the future'	A sun in splendour divided per bend by a flash of lightning	Hawk T.2	Fast-jet advanced flying training
16 (Reserve)	'Hidden things are revealed'	Two crossed keys	Tutor	Elementary flying training
17 (Reserve)	'Strive to excel'	A gauntlet	F-35	Test and evaluation
XXIV	'Ready in all things'	A blackcock	Atlas, C-17, Hercules	Operational conversion unit for large transport aircraft
28	'Whatsoever you may do, do'	A fasces in front of a demi-Pegasus	Chinook, Puma	Operational conversion unit
29 (Reserve)	'Energetic and keen'	An eagle preying on a buzzard	Typhoon	Operational conversion unit for Typhoon
41 (Reserve)	'Seek and destroy'	A double-armed cross	Tornado and Typhoon	Test and evaluation
45 (Reserve)	'Through difficulties I arise'	A winged camel	King Air	Multi-engine training
60 (Reserve)	'I strive through difficulties to the sky'	A markhor's head	Griffin	Helicopter training for air force, navy and army aircrew

72 (Reserve)	'Swift'	A swift	Tucano	Basic fast-jet training
100	'Never stir up a hornet's nest'	A skull and crossbones	Hawk T.1	Target-facilities, forward air controller and weapons systems operator training
115 (Reserve)	'Despite the elements'	A hand holding a tiller	Tutor	Instructor training
202 (Reserve)	'Be always vigilant'	A mallard landing	Griffin	Maritime and mountain rescue training
206 (Reserve)	'Naught escapes us'	An octopus	(None permanently assigned)	Heavy aircraft test and evaluation

DID YOU KNOW?

In 1942 a XV Sqn Stirling bomber was given the name MacRobert's Reply, as Lady MacRobert had lost two of her sons in combat and she had provided funds for the aircraft (along with four Hurricanes). Two Stirlings bore the name during the war and in 1982 it was applied to one of the squadron's Buccaneers. A Tornado then carried the name until the squadron's disbandment in 2017.

NO. 6 FLYING TRAINING SCHOOL

Based around the country, 15 University Air Squadrons and 12 Air Experience Flights give flying experience to university students and Air Cadets under the umbrella of No. 6 Flying Training School, flying the Grob Tutor T.1.

DID YOU KNOW?

Forty-five Maintenance Unit was the first to display a sporran on their official badge. It reflected the unit's origins at Kinloss in Scotland and the safekeeping of the aircraft it was entrusted with.

DID YOU KNOW?

When 23 Sqn's F-4 Phantoms were painted light grey in the 1980s, their unit markings were applied using pastel colours. This led to the squadron being known as the 'Pink Parrots' rather than their preferred 'Red Eagles'.

EAGLE SQUADRONS

During the Battle of Britain several American pilots, such as former Olympian bobsleigh champion Billy Fiske, flew on the British side despite their home country being neutral. They were given their own squadron, number 71, in late 1940. Two others, 121 and 133, were also 'Eagle' squadrons until transferring to the United States Army Air Forces in 1942.

MASCOTS

Several units have adopted animals as mascots.

Squadron	Animal	Details
8 Sqn	Boo Boo (European eagle owl)	Boo Boo was gifted by the Highland Wildlife Park in 1975. His name comes from the species name: Bubo Bubo.
14 Sqn	'Sqn Ldr Eric Aldrovandi' (Burmese python)	Eric was 15 ft 8 in in length and served as mascot for 25 years.
27 Sqn	Gosta (Indian elephant)	The elephant was borrowed from a zoo for a squadron reunion event in 1968.
43 Sqn	Gamecock	The cockerel was adopted when the squadron operated the Gloster Gamecock in the 1920s, and a succession of birds has followed.
65 Sqn	Binder (dog)	Binder was adopted by the squadron during the Battle of Britain and was taken flying by Wing Commander Pat Finucane.
311 (Czech) Sqn	Antis (German shepherd)	Antis was brought to the UK from Europe by Czech pilot Václav Robert Bozděch in 1940. He was later awarded the Dickin Medal (the 'animal VC') for his wartime service, in which he found people trapped in bombed-out buildings.

609 (West Riding) Sqn	Air Commodore William 'Billy' de Goat (goat)	The goat was given to the squadron during the Second World War by the landlady of a local pub. Rank stripes were painted on his horns.
No. 1 School of Technical Training, Halton	Lewis (goat)	In 1944, this Welsh mountain goat became the RAF's first official mascot. He reached the rank of Flt Sgt and, when retired in 1948, was replaced by Lewis II.
No. 1 Radio School, Locking	Hamish McCrackers (Shetland pony)	The pony was adopted by the apprentices at Locking in 1953 and reached the rank of Corporal Aircraft Apprentice.
Recruit Training Sqn, Halton	George (golden Guernsey–Boer goat)	George made his first appearance on parade in 2010.
70 Sqn	Bruneval I (pony)	Bruneval I was given to the squadron in Cyprus by the Parachute Regiment when African horse sickness prevented it returning to the UK.

EXPEDITIONARY AIR WINGS (EAW)

In 2006 EAWs were formed to bring together air and ground elements for deployment overseas. The RAF's outlook had changed after the end of the Cold War and instead of being static and home based (in Germany and in the UK) facing a single perceived threat, it adopted an expeditionary approach.

One of the current wings is 903 EAW, which conducted missions as part of Operation Shader from Akrotiri in Cyprus. It operated Typhoon, Tornado, Voyager, Hercules, Sentry and Sentinel aircraft.

COLOURS AND STANDARDS

Colours and standards have long been a feature of the army but in 1943 King George VI expressed a wish for the RAF to have its own. The flag of the air force, the Ensign featuring a Union Flag and Roundel on a pale blue background, had been approved in 1920 but was only to be flown from a flagpole, not carried on parade from a staff.

COLOURS

The Queen's Colours are 3 ft 9 in. square and made of silk. Each has an RAF-blue coloured background and features the crest of the appropriate establishment or formation along with a Union Flag or royal emblem. Nine have been awarded:

Royal Air Force College Cranwell   1948
Royal Air Force in the United Kingdom   1951
No. 1 School of Technical Training   1952
RAF Regiment   1953
Near East Air Force*   1960
Far East Air Force*   1961
Central Flying School   1969
Royal Auxiliary Air Force   1989
Royal Air Force Halton   1997

*Colours of disbanded formations are laid up in the RAF's central church, St Clement Danes, in London.

STANDARDS

Standards are awarded to squadrons that have operated for 25 years or have carried out 'outstanding operations'. They measure 4 ft x 2 ft 8 in. and are made of silk. The border is composed of the four national flowers of the UK's component countries: leek, rose, shamrock and thistle. The squadron's crest is displayed and up to eight battle honours can also be included (with the exception of those from the interwar period). They can include:

Western Front 1914–18
Home Defence 1916–18
Independent Force and Germany 1914–18
Palestine 1916–18
Iraq 1919–20
Transjordan 1924
North-West Frontier 1930–31
Battle of Britain 1940
Dunkirk
Atlantic 1939–45
Bismarck
Norway 1940
The Dams
Fortress Europe 1940–44
Berlin 1940–45
Arnhem
Normandy 1944
Walcheren
Greece 1940–41
El Alamein
Malta 1940–42
North Africa 1942–43
Gustav Line
Pacific 1941–45
Burma 1944–45
Arctic 1940–45
South Atlantic 1982
Gulf 1991
Kosovo
Iraq 2003

CHAPTER SEVEN

RESERVES AND AUXILIARIES

There is increased emphasis in today's RAF on a mix of regular and reserve personnel, and those in the reserve and auxiliary forces have certainly played an important part in the service through the years.

AUXILIARY AIR FORCE

The Auxiliary Air Force (AAF) was formed in 1924, and squadrons started to be established the following year. It was to be a territorial-type organisation, composed of units based locally around the country with already qualified civilian pilots who were willing to fly in their spare time. There was a certain amount of elitism in membership: 601 Sqn was known as the 'Millionaires' Mob', with an estimated cost of around £50 a year to remain a member, which put it out of the reach of most. The aircraft were supplied by the RAF and maintained by regular ground crew. Auxiliary aircrew played an important part in the Battle of Britain and throughout the rest of the war.

Special Reserve

These units were a mix of regulars and those who had already volunteered and had specialised trades. The pilots were to be trained by the squadron, although some did join who were in fact already qualified to fly. The Special Reserve and AAF shared a common headquarters in London and from 1925 were commanded by Air Commodore Cyril Newall. They were eventually amalgamated into the AAF, although they managed to keep their 500-series squadron numbers.

Auxiliary and Special Reserve squadrons

By 1939 there were 20 AAF and Special Reserve aircraft squadrons. The AAF also had 47 squadrons operating barrage balloons, which were later brought under Balloon Command. All squadrons were brought into the regular air force before the war began. At the outbreak of war in 1939 these were the AAF and Special Reserve squadrons:

Number	Name	Type flown	Role
500	County of Kent	Anson	Maritime patrol
501	County of Gloucester	Hurricane	Fighter
502	Ulster	Anson	Maritime patrol
504	County of Nottingham	Hurricane	Fighter
600	City of London	Blenheim	Fighter
601	County of London	Blenheim	Fighter
602	City of Glasgow	Spitfire	Fighter
603	City of Edinburgh	Spitfire	Fighter
604	County of Middlesex	Blenheim	Fighter
605	County of Warwick	Gladiator/Hurricane	Fighter
607	County of Durham	Gladiator	Fighter
608	North Riding	Anson	Maritime patrol
609	West Riding	Spitfire	Fighter
610	County of Chester	Spitfire	Fighter
611	West Lancashire	Spitfire	Fighter

612	County of Aberdeen	Anson	Maritime patrol
613	City of Manchester	Hind	Army co-operation
614	County of Glamorgan	Hind	Army co-operation
615	County of Surrey	Gladiator	Fighter
616	South Yorkshire	Gauntlet/Battle*	Fighter

*Used for training in preparation for receiving Spitfires.

During the war AAF pilots brought down the first German aircraft over the UK when two Junkers Ju 88s were shot down by aircraft of 602 and 603 Sqns on 16 October 1939 over the Firth of Forth. Five years later the first jet squadron of any Allied air power was an auxiliary unit: 616 Sqn, equipped with Meteors in July 1944.

The AAF was given a Royal prefix in 1947 in recognition of its war service. However, all RAuxAF flying squadrons were disbanded in the 1950s. The Royal Auxiliary Air Force Regiment, which came into existence from the RAF Regiment after the war, was also disbanded. Three squadrons of the RAuxAF Regiment were re-formed in 1979 and further units were established in the years after that. RAuxAF medical personnel took part in Operation Granby.

The RAuxAF, with the Regular Reserves, now forms part of the RAF's Reserve Force. In April 2014 there were 1,720 members of the RAuxAF. At the same time there were 7,120 Regular Reserves (those former full-time personnel).

DID YOU KNOW?

The famous night fighter pilot John 'Cats Eyes' Cunningham was an auxiliary pilot. He flew with 604 (County of Middlesex) squadron and shot down 20 enemy aircraft during the war.

RESERVE OF AIR FORCE OFFICERS (RAFO)

The Reserve of Air Force Officers (RAFO) was created in 1921. It was envisaged that most of the pilots would be those who had served in short service commissions. In order to build up numbers recruitment was aimed at pilots who had flown in the war and civilian commercial pilots. As numbers were not achieved by 1926 (with 489 out of the 700 required), direct recruitment was begun and by 1935 there were 1,500 RAFO pilots.

In order to keep them current, in 1923 and 1924 reserve flying schools were established around the country at Stag Lane, Filton, Renfrew, Whitley and Brough. In 1935 flying training saw changes as parts of the expansion schemes, and civilian schools were designated as elementary and reserve flying training schools (ERFTS). Four of the original reserve flying schools were given ERFTS status. By the beginning of the war there were more than 40 ERFTS, but these were replaced by elementary flying training schools, which carried out all the initial flying training required.

DID YOU KNOW?

Auxiliary and RAFO pilots had to complete a minimum of 12 hours' flying time each year. This was raised to 25 hours in 1935.

RAF VOLUNTEER RESERVE (RAFVR)

'Thank God for the RAFVR.'
AIR CHIEF MARSHAL HUGH DOWDING, AUGUST 1940

The RAFVR was formed as a way of supplying more pilots, and in 1937, it started to enrol civilian men without any previous flying experience. The RAFVR contained men from a wider social range than the more selective Auxiliary Air Force.

When the Second World War began, the RAFVR was the only route into the RAF apart from as apprentices. Not only pilots but observers, gunners, wireless operators and also ground crew were enlisted. RAFVR pilots entered as non-commissioned officers (NCOs), which led to a certain amount of tension with those regular NCOs who had worked their way up over a period of years to reach their rank.

Unlike the AAF, reserve men were not attached to distinct squadrons but were posted wherever needed. Qualified accountants, dentists, engineers, lawyers, doctors or managers could be commissioned as officers to specialise in the appropriate ground branch. Those with languages and abilities that suited interrogation could sign up for intelligence duties.

The RAFVR continued after the war but in 1997 a number of small specialised units were amalgamated into the RAuxAF, with the exception of the RAFVR(T) training branch, which provides officers for Air Cadet squadrons, pilots for Air Cadets' Air Experience Flights and gliding units, and RAFVR(UAS) for University Air Squadron students.

DID YOU KNOW?

Olympic cyclist Sir Chris Hoy was made an Honorary Group Captain in the RAFVR(T) in 2013. TV presenter Carol Vorderman succeeded him in this ambassadorial post for the Air Cadets the following year.

UNIVERSITY AIR SQUADRONS (UAS)

It was felt the RAF would need a supply of officers who had university degrees and so in October 1925 the first two UAS were formed, at Cambridge and Oxford. The number of squadrons was extended by 20 in 1940 as the demand for more pilots increased. Much later, in 1968, the UAS was cut to 16 squadrons, but these continue to allow undergraduates the experience of military flying.

DID YOU KNOW?

Four former UAS members won the Victoria Cross in the Second World War. They included Guy Gibson and Leonard Cheshire, who both commanded 617 Sqn.

CHAPTER EIGHT

WOMEN IN THE SERVICE

ORIGINS

In the First World War women were employed in many jobs from which they had been previously excluded. The need to replace men called up to do military service enabled women to show that they were perfectly capable of fulfilling these roles. It was not just in civilian industries or healthcare that women carried out 'men's work' but also in the military, where women did catering, storekeeping and clerical work as well as driving duties. From a trial period in 1915 their work was expanded in scope, and eventually in 1917 they became formally part of the military structure with the formation of the Women's Auxiliary Army Corps (WAAC).

When the Royal Air Force was formed in April 1918, so too was the Women's Royal Air Force (WRAF). It was not to last as in 1920 the WRAF was disbanded, and it was not until June 1939 that the Women's Auxiliary Air Force (WAAF) was formed from the Auxiliary Territorial Service (the women's equivalent of the Territorial Army), which had been established the year before and included RAF companies.

WARTIME

At the outbreak of war there were less than 2,000 women in the WAAF, and its subsequent vast expansion showed the willingness of women to serve. By the point of its maximum size in 1943, before enrolment was halted by the Ministry of Labour, WAAF personnel amounted to 16 per cent of the RAF.

Year	WAAF personnel
1939 (September)	1,734
1943 (July)	181,835 (peak)

Some men were resistant to the presence of women on airfields and one officer sent his WAAFs off base when enemy aircraft approached. But there were many who regarded women as a welcome addition to service life during wartime.

Women served in 80 different trades, but they were not allowed to fly. Women pilots such as Amy Johnson did fly front-line aircraft during the war, but as civilian members of the Air Transport Auxiliary (ATA) delivering them to front-line units.

Roles carried out by WAAF personnel included:

Administrator
Armourer
Balloon operator
Bomb plotter
Clerk
Cook
Cypher officer
Driver
Electrician
Instrument repairer
Intelligence officer

Mechanic
Medical orderly
Mess orderly
Meteorologist
Photographic interpreter
Policewoman
Radar operator
Radar plotter
Switchboard operator
Tailor
Wireless operator

WHEN THINGS DON'T GO RIGHT: SPITFIRE FLIGHT

One of the tasks undertaken by ground crew was to counterbalance the weight of Spitfires when taxying in high winds by sitting on the tail to prevent the aircraft from tipping over. On 14 February 1945 at Hibaldstow in Lincolnshire, airframe mechanic Margaret Horton achieved a unique distinction by taking to the air as a Spitfire passenger – carried externally! The pilot took off without checking that his 'ballast' had jumped off as normal before he began his take-off run. When in the air he was unaware that Horton was clinging to the tail, but feeling that his controls were sluggish, he came back in for a landing. She jumped off when back on the ground, having suffered a sprained arm, and the pilot, noticing an improvement, took off again. The Spitfire, AB910, is now part of the Battle of Britain Memorial Flight.

WAAF RANKS

In the 1940s WAAF personnel had a different rank structure from their male colleagues.

Ranks (from 1940 to 1948):

Officers	Airwomen
Air Chief Commandant	Warrant Officer
Air Commandant	Flight Sergeant
Group Officer	Sergeant
Wing Officer	Corporal
Squadron Officer	Leading Aircraftwoman
Flight Officer	Aircraftwoman, 1st class
Section Officer	Aircraftwoman, 2nd class
Assistant Section Officer	

They were also paid less, around two-thirds of the amounts earned by their male equivalents.

DID YOU KNOW?

Winston Churchill's daughter served in the WAAF. Sarah Churchill worked as a photographic interpreter at Medmenham. Another famous daughter served in the WAAF and its successor after the war. Jean Conan Doyle, second daughter of Sherlock Holmes writer Arthur, rose through the ranks to become Air Commandant and was Director of the WRAF from 1963 to 1966.

GREAT WOMEN OF THE AIR FORCE

Joan Mortimer, Elspeth Henderson, Helen Turner and Avis J. Hearn

Joan Mortimer joined the WAAF in April 1939. She was posted to Biggin Hill and was there during the Battle of Britain in 1940. At the end of August and beginning of September the airfield came under heavy German attack. During one raid Mortimer was in the dangerous environs of the station's armoury but remained at her post on the telephone switchboard passing on messages. With the attack over, but before the 'all clear' signal, she went out on to the airfield to place red flags next to craters containing unexploded bombs, to warn the airfield's returning fighters. When one exploded, she carried on. For her actions Mortimer was awarded the Military Medal. Two other Military Medals were awarded for the actions of WAAF personnel at Biggin Hill during this period.

Corporal Elspeth Henderson was on duty when the operations room suffered a direct hit but she continued in communication with Uxbridge group headquarters. Sergeant Helen Turner was a switchboard operator at the operations room and continued with her work during the raid. Both Henderson and Turner only left their positions when ordered to do so as fire had broken out.

These three women were the first WAAFs to be awarded the Military Medal out of six in total during the war. Another was Corporal Avis J. Hearn, who during a raid at Poling radar station on 18 August 1940 continued to report enemy bomber positions while under heavy attack. She was asked by another station if she was aware of the bombers' position. She replied: 'The course of the enemy bombers is only too apparent to me because the bombs are almost dropping on my head.'

Constance Babington Smith

Constance Babington Smith led a section in the Central Interpretation Unit at Medmenham and it was there in 1943 that she was to make an important contribution to the war effort. There had been reports of launch sites being prepared in France and intensive efforts were being made to find what type of machine would be using them. Studying aerial reconnaissance photographs taken at Peenemünde on Germany's Baltic coast she spotted a machine sitting on a length of rail. It was found to be a new weapon: a V1 'flying bomb'. Peenemünde was subsequently targeted by Allied bombers. Babington Smith had also noticed an unusual tail-less aircraft that was later identified as the Messerschmitt Me 163 rocket fighter. She was mentioned in dispatches and in 1945 was awarded the MBE. After the war she became a writer, with her first book being an account of photographic interpretation during the war.

POST-WAR

After the war ended, numbers were sharply reduced and 100,000 had left by the middle of 1946. The need for women to remain a part of the service led to the re-formation of the WRAF in 1949. Women could now forge full-time careers as opposed to serving only as temporary personnel.

In 1962 women could become aircrew through the Air Quartermaster category, and in 1968 ranks for men and women were standardised. In 1970 Cranwell received its first female entrants. In 1994 the WRAF was abolished and women were fully integrated into the RAF and by 2015, 94 per cent of roles were open to women, the highest figure amongst the three armed services.

In today's service women can join any branch apart from the RAF Regiment, although in 2016 it was announced that the exclusion of women in ground close combat roles was to be lifted.

FEMALE FIRSTS

Operational station commander	1982	Gp Capt Joan Hopkins took command of air defence radar station RAF Neatishead.
Pilot	1991	Flt Lt Julie Gibson flew Andovers and Hercules and later became the first female captain of an aircraft.
Navigator	1991	Fg Off Anne-Marie Dawe later commanded 54(R) Sqn at Waddington.
Fast-jet pilot	1994	Flt Lt Jo Salter joined 617 Sqn flying the Tornado GR.1.
Fast-jet navigator	1994	Flt Lt Elaine Taylor joined 25 Sqn flying the Tornado F.3.
Squadron commander	2002	Sqn Ldr Nicky Smith took charge of 84 Sqn in Cyprus. Smith had been the first female helicopter pilot, flying search-and-rescue Sea Kings with 22 and 202 Sqns.
First Distinguished Flying Cross	2008	Flt Lt Michelle Goodman became the first woman to be awarded the DFC for flying a casevac mission in Basra while under enemy fire.
Red Arrows pilot	2009	Flt Lt Kirsty Moore became Red 3.
Two-star rank	2013	AVM Elaine West and AVM Sue Gray were appointed.
Squadron commander (fast-jet)	2015	Wg Cdr Nikki Thomas took command of 12 Sqn at Marham.

CHAPTER NINE

TRAINING

After the First World War there was pressure on the armed forces to cut expenditure. Sir Hugh Trenchard reduced the size of the air force but focused on elements which would need to be maintained for future requirements. One was training.

AIRCREW

Aircrew training was rudimentary for those entering the service in its early years. It was not unusual to go solo after a couple of hours' dual instruction. The first-ever class at the Central Flying School in 1912 had passed the Royal Aero Club test simply by flying a figure of 8, flying at a height of 150 m (492 ft) and being able to land within 50 m (164 ft) of a designated spot.

Once war began pilots would arrive at their front-line squadron with less than an hour's training on air combat. There was a School of Aerial Gunnery, but one pilot, Lieutenant James Cross, related how he was there for two days instead of the two weeks the course was meant to last. The high casualty rate of aviators (the life expectancy on the Western Front of an Allied pilot was 11 days) meant there was a need to rush pilots and observers to the front, which overrode training requirements.

In 1936 Training Command was established and proceeded to administer both flying and ground trades, though in 1940 these were separated into Flying Training and Technical Training Commands. Just as with the previous conflict, once war began, the race to get pilots ready for operational duties meant speeding up the process. In the Operational Training Units the course would normally last six weeks; during the Battle of Britain this was reduced to two weeks with the ground school element omitted altogether. Gunnery practice was not always carried out as part of the itinerary of a trainee pilot. Pilots could arrive at a front-line squadron having never fired an aircraft's guns. The situation was worsened by the need for experienced instructors to leave the training units to fly in the front-line squadrons. If new pilots survived their first few days they would hope to learn on the job from the experienced colleagues on their squadrons.

Pilot progression (from 1941)

- ► Initial Training Wing (eight weeks' ground instruction)

- ► Elementary Flying Training School (10 weeks' ground instruction and flying lessons)

- ► Service Flying Training School (16 weeks' advanced flying)

- ► Operational Training Unit (4–6 weeks on a specific aircraft type).

As demand was high, many aircrew were trained in Canada, Australia, New Zealand, Rhodesia or South Africa as part of the Empire Air Training Scheme (later called the British Commonwealth Air Training Plan). Aircrew were also trained in the USA (though its Commonwealth status had long expired!). In 1943 there were 333 flying training schools in use for RAF personnel.

⇜ MY RAF ⇝

SIR ROGER AUSTIN
Air Marshal, served 1957–97

I joined the air force because I was fascinated by aeroplanes and wanted to fly them for a living. Military aeroplanes seemed far more capable and exciting than commercial types.

My initial training lasted for three months (at RAF South Cerney) and was very concentrated. In addition to academic subjects, leadership training, drill and physical training, we learned about the service. Most of it was new to us and we worked hard. It was a fairly exciting time with the prospect of flying in the near future.

Basic flying training was conducted on the Percival Provost T.1 at RAF Syerston and lasted for nine months. It was obviously hard work but I enjoyed it hugely. The Provost had an Alvis Leonides engine of 550 hp, so it was powerful for a basic trainer. Advanced training (at RAF Swinderby) introduced us to the de Havilland Vampire, our first experience of jet aeroplanes. The course lasted for nine months and the pressurised Vampire would go much higher and much faster than the Provost.

Throughout all this training, we were very conscious that a lot of would-be pilots fell by the wayside and we were desperately keen not to join this disappointed group.

I have worked with some memorable characters. During my basic flying training I was fortunate to have Flight Sergeant McTavish as my instructor. He was a granite-faced Scot with a twinkle in his eye and he coped with me superbly; my constant aim was to give him no cause for criticism. He taught me so much about flying and he helped me to grow up. I could not have had a better tutor for those early times.

I was also helped by (the then) Squadron Leader Max Bacon, my first squadron commander on 20 Sqn flying the Hawker Hunter FGA.9 at RAF Tengah in Singapore from 1964–66. He encouraged me and did not overreact to my wilder tendencies.

Apart from the obvious point about flying high-performance aeroplanes for a living (and getting paid for it), I greatly enjoyed the friendship of those I worked with. They were a wonderful bunch of people who worked hard and knew how to enjoy their off-duty times. I find it difficult to think of anyone in the service whom I did not like.

My abiding memory of being in the service must be that in 39 years and about 14 different jobs, plus 12 years flying in the Reserve, I never found myself doing something I did not enjoy – even in the Ministry of Defence. I spent time in many countries throughout Europe, the Mediterranean, the Far East and South America, and I worked with some outstanding people, not only in the Royal Air Force but also in the navy, the army and the civil service.

DID YOU KNOW?

The RAF was the first air force in the world to use only jets for pilot training, when in 1957 the Jet Provost took over as the basic training aircraft.

MODERN-DAY ROUTE

The general route from entrant to fully fledged squadron pilot has not changed much over the decades. A careful selection process sees aptitude tests, selection interviews, health and fitness tests, then pre-recruit training, before acceptance. All pilots in the RAF are officers, and so the first steps in uniform are at the Initial Officer Training at RAF College Cranwell. Once this has been completed, they move to flying training.

The trainee is led through a succession of stages by instructors who introduce new elements as the pupil advances. If a pupil falters, they are given encouragement to overcome whatever issue is of concern. But if unable to do so, they are removed from pilot training and moved to another flying category or to one of the ground-based branches.

The prospective pilot goes through the following stages, with each one combining flying with ground schooling:

Elementary flying training

After flying the Grob Tutor, successful trainees are then streamed to one of three next stages: fast-jet, multi-engine or rotary (helicopter):

Fast-jet training

- ► Initial basic fast-jet training on the Tucano T.1 at Linton-on-Ouse, following which the RAF wings are awarded

- ► Tactical weapons training (Hawk)

- ► Operational Conversion Unit (Typhoon).

Multi-engine

- ► Beechcraft King Air at Cranwell, following which the RAF wings are awarded

- ► Operational Conversion Unit (C-17, Hercules, Atlas).

Rotary

- ▶ Squirrel and Griffin at RAF Shawbury, following which the RAF wings are awarded

- ▶ Operational Conversion Unit (Chinook, Puma).

Pilots then are posted to their squadron to begin the operational part of their flying careers.

SIMULATORS

Technology has played its part in providing 'synthetic' flying training. During the Second World War, the *Link* trainer helped instruct pilots in instrument flying. While mounted on the ground, the trainer could move in the pitch, yaw and roll axes in response to the pilot's control inputs which activated bellows beneath the 'blue box'. Bomber crews also had a crew procedure trainer that could simulate a whole mission, with special effect gunfire, searchlights and engine noise to increase realism.

Modern simulators incorporate full motion, with an immersive visual element, allowing a realistic environment for flying training. The early *Link* trainers had no visual aspect but computer-generated graphics are now projected on to screens above and in front of the modern simulator. One application is display pilots can test their routines without any risk before taking them into the air.

Another innovation in training has been the use of realistic scenarios, monitored through electronic means. Aircraft carry data-link pods to give a real-time depiction of their air-to-air combat, which is viewed on the ground. The air combat manoeuvring instrumentation (ACMI) range at Decimomannu in Sardinia is used for this purpose and on a bigger scale in the USA where crews take part in the Red Flag exercise at Nellis Air Force Base. At the Electronic Warfare Tactics Range at Spadeadam in Cumbria aircrew face simulated radar and SAM threats.

CRANWELL

> *'It is not sufficient to make the Air Force officer a chauffeur and nothing more.'*
> **TRENCHARD MEMORANDUM, DECEMBER 1919**

The RAF College at Cranwell opened on 5 February 1920, a date now known as 'Founder's Day'. It was designed to train men as officers, to teach them how to fly and to instil in them the spirit of the service – to be the air force's equivalent of the army's Sandhurst and the navy's Dartmouth.

The station had already been used by the RNAS during the First World War for training its pilots and observers when it was known as HMS Daedalus. When the air force took over, it became RAF Station Cranwell and the Boys' Wing (to train mechanics and riggers) and flying training school were retained. The addition of a training school for radio operators was also carried out in 1918. This was retained until 1952 when it moved to Locking in Somerset.

The Boys' Wing was replaced by an apprentice school, and apprentices were trained at Cranwell until Halton took over all apprentice training (apart from radio operators) in 1927.

DID YOU KNOW?

The first member of the Royal Family to be in the RAF was Prince Albert (the future King George VI). He had been in the RNAS at Cranwell until the RAF came into being, when he began wearing the light blue uniform. He spent two years at the station as an instructor.

At first cadets were taught in huts, some of which remained in use until three decades later. They were taught for two years and the fees cost the cadets (or their families) up to £75 a year.

The permanent college building that remains today was completed in 1933. The design of College Hall was influenced by Christopher Wren's Royal Hospital at Chelsea and has an 800 ft frontage. Graduation parades are held in front of the College Hall and are accompanied by a fly-past, although at one in the 1980s when two F-4 Phantoms performed the ceremonial duties, one of them flew so low it blew many cadets' hats off.

Cranwell currently carries out elementary and advanced training for pilots and weapons systems operators. It also runs special entrant and re-entrant courses for those officers entering the medical, dental, legal and chaplains branches.

DID YOU KNOW?

Reputedly, Cranwell wasn't targeted by the Luftwaffe during the Second World War as the head of the German air force, Hermann Goering, wanted to use it as his headquarters.

RAF TRADITIONS

Cranwell Carpet

Cadets at Cranwell are not permitted to walk on the carpet under the rotunda in College Hall until they graduate.

CENTRAL FLYING SCHOOL

A Central Flying School (CFS) was established in May 1912 at Upavon to train RFC pilots of both wings: Military (Army) and Naval, although the navy later went its own way with its own flying school. One of the pilots on the first course (alongside the future Lord Trenchard) was Major Robert Smith-Barry who was instrumental in introducing improved training methods. He proposed that instructors should teach trainee pilots in how to cope with difficult flight conditions such as spins, in order to recover successfully, rather than telling them to avoid them as had been done previously. He also advocated using dual controls – something taken for granted now – and introduced two-way communications between student and pupil while in the air. His 'Gosport System' of instruction (named after the airfield where he commanded No. 1 (Reserve) Sqn) was adopted worldwide. In 1919, when Trenchard outlined his plans for the future service, he saw the CFS as where RAF pilots would be trained to be instructors, and so it has continued. It is the world's oldest flying school.

TRAINING SCHOOLS

The RFC had begun with pilots and a few observers (if the aircraft were powerful enough to carry both), but as aircraft grew in size the crews required also increased in number. Until the war, observers would manage the navigation, bomb aiming, photography and aerial gunnery tasks, so in order to train the wireless operators, air gunners, navigators, etc., in the many skills required, the RAF created numerous schools. Some included:

- ► No. 1 Air Gunners School

- ► No. 1 School of Aerial Navigation and Bomb Dropping

- ► No. 1 School of General Reconnaissance

- ► No. 1 Torpedo Refresher School

- ► No. 2 Air Signallers School

- ▶ No. 2 Electrical and Wireless School

- ▶ No. 2 Marine Observers School

- ▶ No. 2 School of Aerial Fighting

- ▶ No. 3 Radio Direction Finding School

- ▶ School of Army Co-operation.

PARACHUTE TRAINING

The Central Landing School was formed in 1940 to train the UK's airborne troops. It was named No. 1 Parachute Training School in 1944 and in May 1969 saw its millionth drop. The school trains airborne troops and others, satisfying a requirement for parachute training that exists in both the navy and the army. The student is awarded their parachute wings after nine successful jumps. Static line jumping is also taught. The school's Specialist Training Squadron instructs UK Special Forces personnel in how to freefall from greater altitudes.

DID YOU KNOW?

Training for parachutists in the 1920s was completed by jumping off a Vickers Virginia biplane bomber – not from the fuselage, as is normal in present-day practice, but from the trailing edge of the outer wing. Trainees would stand on the wing, pull the ripcord, the parachute would open and the slipstream would quickly pull the jumper off the wing to begin their descent.

GROUND TRADES

The establishment of Halton at the very start of the air force's existence was to ensure a tradition of highly skilled and trained personnel. Training centres were provided for all trades, which required frequent changes to keep pace with technological advancement, such as the movement from wooden construction to metal, and the increasing complexity of avionics.

Their expansion during the 1930s is reflected in the numbers enrolled. At Halton in 1935 there were 550 apprentices. The following year this had increased to 916, and in 1936 the figure reached 1,250. The war saw further expansion and by its end, when almost two million men and women had served, seven out of ten had been in ground trades.

A recruit of the time would experience initial training of 8–12 weeks of drill, barrack cleaning and instruction in a variety of topics, all under close scrutiny by NCOs. The next stage might last for only a few weeks for those more unskilled trades, while others in the more specialised areas might be trained for up to two years.

In wartime training had to be carried out wherever it was possible, with civilian garages being utilised for mechanical trades and the General Post Office and BBC training those selected for signals and radar trades. Those enlisting with existing skills were moved quickly through the initial training before being posted to their units.

HALTON

'There is no doubt at all, in my opinion, that Halton and the Halton spirit has been a pillar of strength to the Royal Air Force all over the world. The Halton-trained men have provided the nucleus on which the great expansion of the Air Force was centred.'

LORD TRENCHARD, 6 DECEMBER 1944, HOUSE OF LORDS

Like Cranwell, Halton had a military heritage, being used for training army soldiers during the First World War before the RFC took over with the School of Technical Training (Men). By November 1918, 1,700 instructors were training:

► 6,000 men

► 2,000 women

► 2,000 boys.

The boys were the predecessors of the Halton Apprentices (sometimes known as 'Trenchard's Brats') a key element of the newly established RAF's training structure. Apprentices would be aged between 15½ and 17 and Trenchard thought Halton was ideal for training them, as it was near London and its rail hubs, making it easier for parents and friends to visit during an apprentice's three years of training.

Apprentices arrived at Halton's No. 1 School of Technical Training in 1922; over 40,000 were trained until the apprentice scheme was ended in 1993. Halton is still used today for training not only RAF but also army and navy personnel as well as civilians.

DID YOU KNOW?

The inventor of the jet engine, Sir Frank Whittle, began his RAF career as an apprentice. In 1926 he received a cadetship to go on to officer training. In 1949, while addressing students, he said:

'Though I don't say that if I had not got my cadetship there would have been no jet engine, there certainly wouldn't have been a Whittle jet engine.'

STAFF COLLEGE

The RAF Staff College opened at Andover on 4 April 1922, with 20 students. It was intended to prepare officers with the necessary skills in administration and policy that would be used in the Air Ministry or at headquarters. It was essential for those officers intending to progress to higher command. The Staff College later moved to Bracknell but closed in 1997 when its functions moved to the Joint Services Command and Staff College at Shrivenham.

CHAPTER TEN

AIR CADETS

Venture Adventure

MOTTO OF THE AIR TRAINING CORPS

The Air Training Corps (ATC) was formed in 1941. It was the successor to the Air Defence Cadet Corps (ADCC), founded in 1938 by Air Commodore Adrian Chamier, who wished to see an organisation for young men interested in aviation, who could be potential recruits for the RAF or Fleet Air Arm (FAA). With this in mind cadets were provided with uniforms and taught drill. Discipline was enforced. They were given talks on aviation and life in the air forces.

There were two types: 'school' squadrons composed of pupils and former pupils, and 'open' types that recruited from the local community. The first 50 squadrons that formed were given dispensation to add the suffix 'F' after their squadron number, standing for 'Founder' squadron, which is retained by current units.

When the Second World War began the ADCC carried out preliminary training for those about to enter the RAF or FAA. The government took control of the organisation, which then became the Air Training Corps on 5 February 1941. There was keen interest and by 1942 there were 210,000 cadets. At the end of the war it was taken under the wing of the air force as part of Reserve Command. In 1967 its Royal Warrant was amended; its stated aims are:

1. To promote and encourage amongst young people a practical interest in aviation and the RAF.

2. To provide training which will be useful both in the services and in civilian life.

3. To foster the spirit of adventure, and to develop the qualities of leadership and good citizenship.

A major part of the cadet experience was flying, and gliding provided a simple and cost-effective way of giving cadets their first experience in the air. Eighty-four gliding schools had been formed at RAF stations by 1946. Powered flying, which had been carried out by taking cadets up in RAF aircraft, was complemented by air experience flights, operating the de Havilland Chipmunk. In 1999 the flights were incorporated into the University Air Squadron organisation, which flies the Grob Tutor.

DID YOU KNOW?

During national service, cadets who had been awarded their proficiency certificates were guaranteed entry into the RAF as tradesmen.

The ATC now forms part of Royal Air Force Air Cadets, along with the Combined Cadet Force (RAF). There are over 40,000 air cadets in over 1,000 squadrons around the country. The cadet organisation had been male-only until in 1980 it was made possible for girls to join. In 2017 the commandant was Air Commodore Dawn McCafferty. Cadets are supervised by volunteer Civilian Instructors and in uniform by adult Warrant Officers and officers in the RAFVR (Training) although in January 2017 it was announced that a new commission had been created for officers of all UK cadet forces.

Activities available to cadets:

- ▶ Duke of Edinburgh Award Scheme
- ▶ Shooting
- ▶ Sports (Seven major sports promoted are: athletics, cross-country running, football, rugby, hockey, netball and swimming)
- ▶ Aircraft recognition
- ▶ Canoeing
- ▶ Hillwalking
- ▶ Camping
- ▶ Sailing
- ▶ Skiing.

Cadets are also offered the opportunity to attend summer camps at current RAF stations.

Cadets are a common sight at airshows, where they assist with the running of the events, through helping with car park marshalling or selling show programmes. At the Royal International Air Tattoo at Fairford they take part in the post-show 'FOD plod', which is when the airfield is manually checked to collect any pieces of rubbish which could be ingested into aircraft air intakes and cause foreign object damage (FOD).

FAMOUS MEMBERS OF THE ATC

Danny Blanchflower	Footballer
Richard Burton	Actor
Gary Numan	Musician
Geoff Capes	Weightlifter and shot-putter
Linford Christie	Athlete
Timothy Dalton	Actor
John Conteh	Boxer
Michael Foale	Astronaut
Robson Green	Actor
Patrick Moore	Astronomer
Len Deighton	Writer
Tom Fletcher	Musician (McFly)
Mike Nicholson	TV war reporter
Chris Ryan	Soldier (SAS) and writer
Alan Sillitoe	Writer
Rory Underwood	Rugby player

CHAPTER ELEVEN

PUBLIC FACE OF THE RAF

The importance of presenting the public with a good impression of the RAF's work and personnel has always been appreciated by its commanders. It helps recruitment but in its early years was also vital in helping safeguard the future of this new organisation which did not have universal support amongst other branches of the armed forces.

AIRSHOWS

In July 1920 the RAF held its first Aerial Pageant at Hendon in north London, which drew a crowd of 60,000. Until they ended in 1937, the Hendon displays were used as a showcase of the air force's prowess in the skies. Displays included:

▶ Formation flying – Armstrong Whitworth Siskins and Hawker Furies were flown attached together with rubber cords; they flew their entire display without breaking the connections

▶ Aerial refuelling demonstrations

► 'Crazy flying' displays by Avro 504Ns in which the biplanes were thrown around as if out of control

► Sky-writing – 'RAF' was written in the skies at the 1932 show

► Climbing competitions by Siskins

► Mock air-to-air combat – one display saw the two-engined Boulton Paul Sidestrand performing aerobatics to escape its fighter attackers

► Gunnery demonstrations – a balloon in the shape of a goose was shot down at one show

► The catapulting of a Vickers Virginia bomber into the air in a distance of just 100 ft

► Recreation of torpedo attacks by Blackburn Darts

► Set-piece attacks – the 1922 Pageant featured bombers attacking a mock-up fortress of the 'Wottnot' tribe.

Following the end of the Hendon shows, the RAF continued with its Empire Air Days, which allowed the public into airbases to see the latest machines in action. After the Second World War, 'At Home' displays were held around Battle of Britain Day on 15 September. Showing the size of the air force at the time, in 1951 66 stations were opened to the public. The last At Home display was held in 2013 at RAF Leuchars, before the base became an army base.

RED ARROWS

The Red Arrows are one of the world's current premier aerobatic teams. Post-war there were many jet formation teams, one of which was the Yellow Jacks, established in 1964, which flew the Folland Gnat two-seat trainer. When the jets were painted red – the official colour of training aircraft of the day – the team soon became the Red Arrows.

The Gnats were replaced by the BAe Hawk T.1 in time for the 1980 season. Based at Scampton in Lincolnshire, the nine jets carry out around 80 displays in the UK and abroad during the airshow summer season. They regularly perform two displays a day, sometimes at opposite ends of the country. Pilots are full-time members of the team and spend three years wearing the famous red flying suit.

The team perform aerobatic manoeuvres as a nine-ship and then break into separate sections. Each pilot is known not by name but by his number in the formation, so for example, Red 1 is the team's leader – on the ground and in the air. Reds 1 to 5 form 'Enid' (after Enid Blyton's Famous Five) and Reds 6 to 9 are known as 'Gypo'. (The commentator at each show, and who flies the spare aircraft, is known as Red 10.)

The Red Arrows practise three different shows – full, rolling and flat – any of which can be performed on a given day depending on the weather. The 2016 full display contained the following formations, some of which are carried out by the Synchro Pair, which fly some of the most dynamic elements of the show, namely, flying towards each other in opposition manoeuvres down to 100 ft above the ground.

Red Arrows formations:

Apollo	Gypo Pass	Shotgun
Big Vixen	Hammerhead Break	Shuttle
Carousel	Heart and Spear	Slalom
Corkscrew	Mirror	Swan
Cyclone	Opposition Barrel	Tornado
Double Rolls	Python	Twister
Fred	Revolution	Typhoon
Goose	Rollbacks	Vixen Break
Gypo Break	Short Diamond	Wall

THE FALCONS

The RAF's parachute display team is based at Brize Norton. The team, which was formed in 1961, is composed of parachute instructors who spend three years performing public displays.

As with other display teams the Falcons have different shows for different weather conditions. The High Show sees the team jump at 12,000 ft, freefall and then form up in a vertical stack. The lowest display begins at 2,500 ft above the ground. The Falcons jump from Puma and Chinook helicopters and C-130 Hercules.

BATTLE OF BRITAIN MEMORIAL FLIGHT

In the 1950s it was felt by veterans that the Battle of Britain should be commemorated through a historic aircraft flight. Hurricanes and Spitfires were collected and in 1973 the fighters were joined by an Avro Lancaster. Its arrival widened the scope of the flight to mark the contribution and sacrifice of aircrew in all commands during the war.

DID YOU KNOW?

Spitfire IIA P7350 is the only Spitfire flying anywhere in the world that took part in the Battle of Britain.

Currently the flight has the following aircraft:

Aircraft	Registration
Lancaster	PA474
Hurricane IIC	LF363, PZ865
Spitfire IIA	P7350

Spitfire VB	AB910
Spitfire IX	MK356
Spitfire XVI	TE311
Spitfire PR.19	PM631, PS915
Dakota	ZA947*
Chipmunk	WG486, WK518**

*Used for familiarisation training and as a display aircraft.
**Used for continuation training.

DISPLAY AIRCRAFT

Depending on operational requirements and resources available the airshow season can see other aircraft from the air force's inventory perform displays. A reduced number of types in the inventory compared with previous years means there is less opportunity for the public to see RAF aircraft on show, but types such as the Typhoon, Hawk, Chinook, Tutor and Tucano have been flown in recent years. Role demos are sometimes carried out with Tornadoes and Hawks.

RAF MUSEUM

The RAF Museum operates two sites: Hendon, which opened in 1972, and Cosford in 1979. Hendon's collection of historic aircraft contains many examples of the aircraft types flown by the air force. One of these is Avro Lancaster R5868 'S-Sugar', which flew 139 operational missions during the Second World War. (Lancasters were only expected to last 21 missions on average.) It also displays Luftwaffe aircraft captured at the end of the Second World War. A main feature at Cosford is the National Cold War Exhibition, which features all three V-bombers.

BANDS

Another aspect of the public-facing side of the RAF is its musical bands, which were formed to increase public knowledge of the air force and also to provide entertainment for the RAF's own personnel.

The RAF School of Music was created in July 1918, around the time the 'Royal Air Force March Past' was composed. The Central Band came into being two years later and still performs to this day. In 1923 it was the first UK military band to be broadcast on the radio. The Second World War saw an expansion, and a new trade of Aircrafthand/Musician was created for forming dance bands at stations around the country. Secondary duties are part of the musician's responsibilities, and almost 200 served as medical orderlies in the 1991 Gulf War.

DID YOU KNOW?

The RAF Symphony Orchestra played for Stalin, Truman and Churchill at the Potsdam Conference in 1945.

POLICE DOG DEMONSTRATION TEAM

Beginning with the 1948 Royal Tournament, RAF police dogs and their handlers have given public demonstrations. As well as this and other UK events such as the Edinburgh Tattoo, the team also displayed overseas. It is no longer in existence, but displays are sometimes given by part-time volunteers.

RAF BENEVOLENT FUND (RAFBF)

The RAFBF is the service's main welfare charity. After the First World War Lord Trenchard was behind the establishment of the fund to raise money to provide assistance to ex-RAF personnel in need. It also aimed to build a national memorial to those who had died while in the UK's air forces, and it currently maintains and preserves the RAF Memorial in London. In 2015 the RAFBF spent over £18 million supporting 41,500 people.

RAF CHARITABLE TRUST

The Trust aims to support projects that will benefit serving personnel, air cadets, other young people and veterans. Its stated mission is to 'promote the Royal Air Force, to support its people now and into the future and to encourage air-mindedness and the aviation-related education of youth'. The RAF Charitable Trust Enterprises, which provides most of the funds for the Trust, runs the annual Royal International Air Tattoo held at Fairford each year.

RAF ASSOCIATION (RAFA)

The idea behind the RAFA came from three serving RAF men, who in 1929 wanted to find a way of offering welfare support to serving and former personnel. The following year an organisation was formed called Comrades of the Royal Air Forces Association (the name was shortened in 1943). In 1947 it reached a peak with 200,000 members in over 560 branches, and currently there are 63,500 members in 422 branches. In 2015 RAFA volunteer welfare officers made over 100,000 calls and visits to those in need. It runs an ongoing fundraising campaign called The Wings Appeal.

Individuals also give up their time to take part in fundraising activities, while other charities with links to the RAF have also been set up over time. Following the death in 2011 of Flight Lieutenant Jon Egging while flying with the Red Arrows, a charity was established in his name to support young people in achieving their potential.

PART 3

THE SERVICE

CHAPTER TWELVE

RANKS, BADGES, UNIFORMS AND MEDALS

When the air force was formed it was proposed to use a mixture of navy and army ranks, but this was abandoned when it was pointed out that the senior ranks proposed were navy-derived and junior ones were from the army, which gave altogether the wrong impression. Instead, it was felt that new ones, or existing army ones, should be used.

The various ranks proposed are listed in descending order:

- ▶ Air Marshal

- ▶ Second Ardian*

- ▶ Third Ardian

- ▶ Fourth Ardian

- ▶ Banneret

- ► Reeve
- ► Squadron Leader
- ► Flight Leader
- ► Lieutenant
- ► Ensign.

*Ardian stemmed from the Gaelic words 'àrd' and 'eun' meaning 'high bird'.

These ranks were rejected, so the army ones familiar from the RFC were retained until in 1919 new ranks were introduced that are still in use today:

Rank	Abbreviation	Sleeve insignia
Air Officers		
Marshal of the RAF	MRAF	One thick stripe, four medium stripes
Air Chief Marshal	Air Chf Mshl	One thick stripe, three medium stripes
Air Marshal	Air Mshl	One thick stripe, two medium stripes
Air Vice-Marshal	AVM	One thick stripe, one medium stripe
Air Commodore	Air Cdre	One thick stripe
Group Captain and below		
Group Captain	Gp Capt	Four medium stripes
Wing Commander	Wg Cdr	Three medium stripes
Squadron Leader	Sqn Ldr	Two medium stripes with one thin stripe
Flight Lieutenant	Flt Lt	Two medium stripes

Flying Officer	Fg Off	One medium stripe
Pilot Officer	Plt Off	One thin stripe
Non-Commissioned Aircrew		
Master Aircrew	MAcr	Royal coat of arms above eagle surrounded by laurel wreaths
Flight Sergeant (Aircrew)	Flt Sgt	Crown and eagle above three chevrons
Sergeant (Aircrew)	Sgt	Eagle above three chevrons
Non-Commissioned other ranks		
Warrant Officer	WO	Royal coat of arms
Flight Sergeant	Flt Sgt	Crown above three chevrons
Chief Technician (Technical trades only)	Chf Tech	Four-bladed propeller above three chevrons
Sergeant	Sgt	Three chevrons
Corporal	Cpl	Two chevrons
Lance Corporal (RAF Regiment only)	L Cpl	One chevron
Junior Technician (phased out in 2005 but personnel remain)	Jnr Tech	Four-bladed propeller
Senior Aircraftman (Technical trades only)	SAC Tech	Three-bladed propeller inside circle
Senior Aircraftman/ Aircraftwoman	SAC	Three-bladed propeller
Leading Aircraftman/ Aircraftwoman	LAC	Two-bladed propeller
Aircraftman/ Aircraftwoman	AC/ACW	n/a

UNIFORM AND CLOTHING

BADGES
The RAF badge depicts an eagle set over a circle bearing the air force's motto, 'Per ardua ad astra', with a crown above.

Cap badges
When the RAF was formed in 1918 new cap badges came into existence. The airmen's and NCOs' was very similar to that of the Royal Flying Corps, which was previously worn by officers, NCOs and other ranks. The new badge was a crown above the letters 'RAF' surrounded by a laurel wreath. A Warrant Officer's badge was similar to that worn by commissioned officers.

The officers' badge (below air rank) was different, an embroidered badge with a laurel wreath below an eagle and above them the crown. The air-ranked officers' badge had a lion set above the crown.

These designs are still worn today.

Qualification badges
Those who have qualified in various areas are entitled to wear badges reflecting their status.

Flying and parachuting badges
Badges that can be currently worn (with their initials as depicted on the badge in brackets):

▶ Pilot*

▶ Pilot RPAS

▶ Weapons Systems Officer/Operator

▶ Fighter Controller (FC)

▶ Airborne Technician (AT)

- Image Analyst (IA)

- Qualified Gliding Instructor (G)**

- Parachute Jump Instructor (Granted 'honorary aircrew' status in 1945).**

*A preliminary flying badge is worn by UAS personnel.
**Not worn by frontline aircrew, but still awarded.

Previous brevets, no longer issued:

- Observer (O)

- Navigator (N)

- Air Electronics Officer/Operator (AE)

- Flight Engineer (E)

- Air Loadmaster (LM)

- Air Bomber (B)

- Air Gunner (AG)

- Wireless Operator (Air) (S)

- Meteorological Observer (M)

- Observer (Radio) (RO)

- Air Quartermaster (QM).

DID YOU KNOW?

The badge worn by pilots depicts the wings of a swift. The wings worn by the RFC pilots were the first in the world to be awarded to display a pilot's qualified status.

RAF TRADITIONS

Pilot's wings

It is a tradition that when a pilot's wings are sewn onto the breast of their uniform, a shilling coin is placed behind the centre. The origins of the tradition, which began in the Second World War, are unknown.

Other qualification badges

Other badges are worn by non-aircrew personnel:

- ▶ Parachutist (with or without wings)
- ▶ Special Forces Parachutist
- ▶ All Arms Commando Dagger
- ▶ Cabin Crew (CC)
- ▶ RAF Paramedic Badge
- ▶ Flight Medical Officer
- ▶ Flight Nursing Officer
- ▶ Flight Nurse
- ▶ Flight Nursing Attendant
- ▶ Mountain Rescue
- ▶ Explosive Ordnance Disposal
- ▶ Marksman
- ▶ Drum Major
- ▶ Voluntary Bandsman.

Branch and trade groups

There are badges to display certain trades or branches:

- RAF medical services

- PMRAFNS nurses

- Dental branch

- Chaplains branch

- RAF Regiment

- RAF Police

- Musician

- Physical training

- Telecommunications

- Royal Auxiliary Air Force

- RAF Volunteer Reserve Training Branch.

DID YOU KNOW?

In the Second World War, pilots in the Desert Air Force who were shot down but made their way back to their airfields were made members of the 'Late Arrivals Club', and a badge featuring a winged flying boot was awarded.

UNIFORMS

In the Royal Flying Corps officers and men had worn a double-breasted tunic derogatorily dubbed the 'maternity jacket'.

The formation of the new air force meant there was a need for a new uniform. In 1918, a pale blue uniform appeared, although it wasn't popular and wasn't in use for long.

The blue-grey colour as used currently was established in 1919, and the Officers' uniforms have not changed markedly since that time.

Airmen's uniforms were initially buttoned up to the collar but were replaced in 1936 with one that allowed a shirt and tie to be worn, in the same manner as officers. Up until the Second World War puttees and breeches were worn but were replaced by slacks. Battle dress was introduced, similar in style to the army's and featuring a blouson jacket. This became No. 2 Home Service Dress. The uniforms were made of heavy serge, although in 1973 this was replaced by a lighter material when a new uniform was introduced.

Current uniforms

These are the main forms of uniform worn by RAF personnel:

No. 1 Service Dress (No. 1 SD)	
Description:	Worn at formal and ceremonial occasions. Ranks of Air Vice-Marshal and above are entitled to wear ceremonial sash and shoulder boards on certain occasions. Brown leather gloves are worn by officers and Warrant Officers. Other ranks wear black leather gloves or white cotton depending on the occasion.
Details:	No. 1 SD hat, tunic jacket, trousers, shirt, black tie, polished shoes. Greatcoat if required. (Turbans may be worn by Sikhs instead of headdress.)
Female personnel:	No. 1 SD tunic has no belt and is worn with trousers or skirt. The No. 1 SD hats are of a different style to that worn by men. Hijabs may be worn under the hat.
No. 2 Service Working Dress (No. 2 SD)	
Description:	Routine working dress.

Details:	Trousers and long-sleeved Wedgwood-blue shirt and black tie, with or without jersey. Ties are not worn with a short-sleeved shirt, unless under a jumper. A No. 1 SD hat, beret or field service cap may be worn. Berets are not worn by officers, unless in the RAF Regiment. A blue leather flying jacket may be worn by officers and NCOs. The zip must be secured no further than 10 cm from the top stop. The blue rain jacket may be worn as outerwear and a shorter, general purpose jacket may be worn, but the jersey must not be visible at the bottom of jacket. No. 2C SD (Restricted Trade) is for certain trades and is a dark blue shirt.
Female personnel:	No. 2 SD is similar to that worn by male personnel, with the addition of a skirt (mid-knee length). Maternity wear is available.

No. 3 Service Dress – operational clothing

Description:	Personal clothing system combat uniform (PCS CU). This is a camouflaged set of clothing worn by male and female personnel. To be worn in operations, operational training and exercises. Regulations and clothing apply equally to male and female personnel.
Details:	A lightweight combat suit (jacket and trousers) is worn, with jacket tucked into trousers. When the combat helmet is not worn as a headdress, a beret is to be worn. The field service cap can be worn by two-star rank officers. T-shirts are worn underneath all year round, and a thermal microfleece shirt is for colder conditions along with a mid-layer fleece garment for under the windproof smock. There is also a lightweight moisture vapour permeable (MVP) suit of waterproof jacket and trousers. Boots are combat assault type and gloves are issued. The outer garment is a camouflaged smock.

No. 4 Service Dress – optional mess dress (No. 4 SD)	
Description:	This mess dress is for officer cadets, most non-regular officers, and airmen and airwomen of any rank.
Details:	The No. 1 SD with the addition of a white shirt and bow tie.

No. 5 Service Dress – mess dress (No. 5 SD)	
Description:	This evening and mess dress is for male officers, Warrant Officers and Senior NCOs for formal occasions such as dining-in nights.
Details:	Short 'Eton' jacket worn with No. 5 SD trousers (for which braces may be used). A white Marcella shirt is worn with gold cufflinks, and a blue waistcoat or a slate-grey cummerbund may also be worn. Unit-specific cummerbunds can be worn at a station commander's discretion. Black bowties are to be worn and shoes must be patent evening shoes. Members of Scottish RAuxAF squadrons are entitled to wear a kilt of the Douglas tartan.
Female personnel:	The No. 5 mess dress sees the wearing of an ankle-length blue-grey skirt. Hand or clutch bags should be black patent and earrings may be worn if plain, spherical and of gold or pearl.

No. 6 Service Dress (warm weather areas) (No. 6 SD)	
Description:	No. 6 SD is worn by all male ranks overseas on formal and ceremonial occasions, and comes in two versions.
Details:	No. 6 SD No. 1 SD hat with No. 6 SD stone-coloured jacket and trousers is worn with a stone-coloured shirt. No. 6A SD A full ceremonial white pocketless jacket and trousers is available for officers of specific appointments or for officers who purchase them at their own expense. The jacket is not worn with a tie and is fully buttoned to the collar. Ranks of Air Vice-Marshal and above can wear a sash.

Female personnel:	The No. 6 SD warm weather stone-coloured service dress is worn by officers and airwomen on all formal occasions when overseas. The No. 6 dress (frock) is worn as a routine working dress. No. 6A SD full ceremonial is a white suit for officers in specific appointments.
No. 7 Service Dress (warm weather areas) (No.7 SD)	
Description:	Stone-coloured routine working dress for warm weather areas.
Details:	The No. 7 SD has long trousers, but shorts form part of No. 7B SD (not to be worn in the Middle East or USA). The long-sleeved shirt is worn with a tie and sleeves that should not be rolled up. Desert boots can replace the black issue shoes. Stone-coloured socks are worn.
Female personnel:	Women can also wear long trousers or shorts.
No. 8 Service Dress (warm weather areas – mess dress) (No.8 SD)	
Description:	Officers are issued with No. 8 SD, while Warrant Officers and Senior NCOs may purchase it at their own expense. It is for formal occasions. An informal version can be used for RAF personnel serving in navy ships or shore bases.
Details:	White 'Eton' jacket with No. 5 SD trousers, cummerbund, white shirt and bow tie.
Female personnel:	Women's dress includes a mess skirt (No. 5 mess dress), and women can wear court or black evening shoes.
No. 9, 10, 11 Service Dress (musicians)	
Description:	Musicians are issued with a variety of uniform items, which include a ceremonial peaked cap and different styles of tunic and cape. Accessories such as aiguillettes, shoulder knots and sashes can be worn by the relevant personnel. Musicians are also provided with warm weather clothing.

Female personnel:	The dress for female musicians is identical save for the addition of the skirt and shoe options available.

General instructions

There are also several general instructions issued for uniforms. One is that uniform and civilian clothes are not to be mixed. Uniforms are generally to be worn while on duty or travelling to and from a place of duty and other civilian occasions. Uniforms are not to be worn while personnel are on leave or visiting licensed premises (unless specifically permitted by chain of command), while hitchhiking or as part of any proceedings which might call into question the impartiality of the service.

Specific items

Some items require specific instructions:

Sunglasses	May be worn when deemed necessary.
Poppies	The Royal British Legion Poppy can be worn during the Remembrance period. The paper poppy is to be worn for parades and ceremonial duty, but a small enamel poppy can be worn on working dress and combat uniform.
Mourning bands	Only officers and Warrant Officers are to wear mourning bands. Those below WO rank can only wear bands when at a private funeral. Mourning bands are not to be worn at Remembrance services.
Women's hosiery	The colour should be nearly black when worn with No. 2 SD skirt. When personnel are wearing No. 1 SD, hosiery should be 15 Denier, nearly black in colour. Socks are worn with trousers.
Umbrellas	Black umbrellas can be carried, but not on parade.

Scarves	Plain black scarves may be worn (with No. 2 uniform).
Ballgowns	May be worn for annual mess balls and ladies' guest nights at the discretion of the commanding officer.
Hair	Men's hair is to be 'well cut and trimmed' and if it is dyed it's to be in a uniform shade. Sikhs may keep their hair long and Rastafarians are to ensure that their dreadlocks are worn no longer than the collar. Women are to keep their hair in a neat style, and it is not to be longer than the bottom edge of the jacket collar. Ponytails may be worn when breathing apparatus has to be used.
Beards	Beards are only allowed on medical or religious grounds, but this permission may be removed if a beard prevents breathing apparatus being worn correctly.
Cosmetics	Cosmetics are not to be used, and women must not wear brightly coloured nail varnish.
Jewellery	Men can wear a wedding band and only one other ring. Earrings and thumb rings are not permitted. Women can wear a wedding band, an engagement ring and one other ring. One ear stud may be worn in each ear (not on parades).
Piercings	Piercing jewellery is not to be worn when on duty.
Tattoos	Tattoos must not be visible and are generally discouraged.

Aircrew flying clothing

No. 14 Dress (flying clothing) encompasses the clothing to be worn by all aircrew when on flying duties. Aircrew should not wear flying clothing when on ground administrative duties.

The flying suit is known as No. 14A Dress and is olive drab in colour. It is worn with aircrew vest, green socks, flying boots and gloves. A cold weather flying jacket (No. 14B) is issued along with cold weather trousers. A camouflaged jacket (CS95 or PCS CU) can be worn. A blue leather flying jacket (No. 14C) can be purchased at own expense but is only to be worn on the ground.

DID YOU KNOW?

During the Second World War fighter pilots would indicate their separateness from other branches of the air force by leaving the top button of their tunics undone.

MEDALS

Various medals are currently available with some awarded to other military personnel and some specifically for actions in the air.

GALLANTRY AND MERITORIOUS SERVICE MEDALS

Victoria Cross (VC)

Instituted:	1856
Ribbon:	Crimson
Medal:	Bronze
Inscription:	'For Valour'
Level:	1

Created in 1856, the VC is the highest award for members of the British armed forces, given for gallantry in the face of enemy fire.

Fifty-one of the 1,358 VCs have been awarded to aircrew. Fifteen were awarded to members of the RFC while four RAF personnel were awarded it in the First World War, beginning a tradition of bravery that would be continued in the Second World War. These awards were to aircrew in the air force or in Commonwealth air forces under the command of the RAF, such as the Royal Australian Air Force (RAAF), Royal New Zealand Air Force (RNZAF), Royal Canadian Air Force (RCAF) and South African Air Force (SAAF).

Name (Pilot unless stated)	Squadron	Aircraft	Date of action	Details
First World War				
Captain Freddie West	8	Armstrong Whitworth FK.8	10 August 1918	Continued reconnaissance while injured.
Major George Barker	201	Sopwith Snipe	27 October 1918	Fought dogfight while injured.
Captain Andrew Beauchamp Proctor	84	SE.5a	8 October 1918	For sustained effort.
Major Edward Mannock*	85	SE.5a	(Killed 28 July 1918)	For sustained effort.
Second World War				
Flying Officer Donald Garland*	12	Fairey Battle	12 May 1940	Bombed bridges in Belgium.
Sergeant Thomas Gray (observer)*	12	Fairey Battle	12 May 1940	Bombed bridges in Belgium.
Flight Lieutenant Roderick Learoyd	49	Handley Page Hampden	12 August 1940	Bombing raid on Dortmund–Ems Canal.

Flight Lieutenant James Nicolson	249	Hawker Hurricane	16 August 1940	Shot down Me 110 while injured, with aircraft on fire. Only Fighter Command VC of the war.
Sergeant John Hannah (wireless operator/air gunner)	83	Handley Page Hampden	15 September 1940	During bombing raid at Antwerp extinguished a serious fire in the aircraft while sustaining severe burns. At 19, youngest RAF VC awardee.
Flying Officer Kenneth Campbell*	22	Bristol Beaufort	6 April 1941	Carried out a lone torpedo attack on *Gneisenau* at Brest.
Wing Commander Hughie Edwards	105	Bristol Blenheim	4 July 1941	Carried out a low-level daylight bombing raid on Bremen.
Sergeant James Ward (2nd pilot)	75 (New Zealand)	Vickers Wellington	7/8 July 1941	Climbed on to the wing to put out an engine fire during a raid on Münster.
Squadron Leader Arthur King Scarf*	62	Bristol Blenheim	9 December 1941	Flew a lone attack on Singora airfield (Thailand). Landed his aircraft while severely injured.
Squadron Leader John Nettleton	44	Avro Lancaster	17 April 1942	Continued a daylight raid on an engine factory in Augsburg while under heavy fighter attack.
Flying Officer Leslie Manser*	50	Avro Manchester	30 May 1942	Killed after ensuring his crew escaped from stricken aircraft.

Flight Sergeant Rawdon 'Ron' Middleton* (RAAF)	149	Short Stirling	28/29 November 1942	Despite being seriously injured, brought aircraft back to UK to allow crew to parachute out.
Wing Commander Hugh Malcolm*	18	Bristol Blenheim	4 December 1942	Killed while leading an attack on German airfield in Tunisia.
Squadron Leader Leonard Trent	487 (RNZAF)	Lockheed Ventura	3 May 1943	Prosecuted attack at Amsterdam when attacked by German fighters.
Wing Commander Guy Gibson	617	Avro Lancaster	16/17 March 1943	Led attack on Ruhr dams.
Flying Officer Lloyd Trigg* (RNZAF)	200	Consolidated Liberator	11 August 1943	Successfully attacked a U-boat in Atlantic off the coast of West Africa.
Flight Sergeant Arthur Aaron*	218	Short Stirling	12 August 1943	Despite being seriously injured by another Stirling's gunfire on raid on Turin, landed damaged bomber in North Africa.
Flight Lieutenant William Reid	61	Avro Lancaster	3 November 1943	Injured in two night fighter attacks, continued to bomb target then brought damaged aircraft back.
Pilot Officer Cyril Barton*	578	Handley Page Halifax	30/31 March 1944	Hit by night fighters on way to Nuremberg, carried on to target. Died on crash landing back in UK.

Sergeant Norman Jackson (flight engineer)	106	Avro Lancaster	26 April 1944	Climbed onto the wing to put engine fire out. Was injured and thrown off the wing in a second night fighter attack. Parachuted and then captured.
Pilot Officer Andrew Mynarski (air gunner)*	419 (RCAF)	Avro Lancaster	12/13 June 1944	With aircraft on fire, Mynarski attempted to free trapped rear gunner, who subsequently survived the crash.
Flight Lieutenant David Hornell*	162 (RCAF)	Consolidated Canso	24 June 1944	In successfully attacking U-boat north of Shetland aircraft was damaged and forced to land on the sea. Crew took to dinghy and Hornell led his men in holding on until rescued after 20 hours on the sea.
Flight Lieutenant John Cruickshank	210	Consolidated Catalina	17 July 1944	Continued successful attack on U-boat while wounded and aircraft badly damaged.
Squadron Leader Ian Bazalgette	635	Avro Lancaster	4 August 1944	After aircraft set on fire during bombing run, ordered crew to bale out. With two wounded still on board attempted to crash-land the stricken Lancaster but it exploded and all were killed.

Wing Commander Leonard Cheshire	102, 35, 1652 (Heavy Conversion Unit), 76, 617	Whitley, Halifax, Lancaster, Mosquito, Mustang	8 September 1944 (Gazetted)	For sustained effort.
Flight Lieutenant David Lord*	271	Douglas Dakota	19 September 1944	During resupply mission to Arnhem aircraft was hit. Ordered crew to bale out before crashing. Only Transport Command VC of the war.
Squadron Leader Robert Palmer*	109	Avro Lancaster	23 December 1944	On his 111th sortie, aircraft was hit and two engines put out of action on run in to drop target markers on Cologne. Continued bombing run before aircraft crashed.
Flight Sergeant George Thompson (wireless operator/air gunner)	9	Avro Lancaster	1 January 1945	When aircraft set on fire during raid on Dortmund–Ems Canal, aided two crew members despite being seriously burnt.
Captain Edwin Swales (SAAF)*	582	Avro Lancaster	23 February 1945	As Master Bomber over Pforzheim aircraft badly damaged by night fighter but continued until aircraft was no longer flyable. Ordered crew to bale out, before dying in ensuing crash.

*Posthumous award

George Cross (GC)

Instituted: 1940
Ribbon: Dark blue
Medal: Solid silver, with St George slaying the dragon in centre
Inscription: 'For Gallantry'
Level: 1

The second-highest award in the UK, the George Cross is predominantly awarded to civilians (and famously to citizens of Malta in 1942) but can be awarded to military personnel who carry out acts of extreme bravery away from enemy action. Thirty-three RAF personnel have been awarded the George Cross.*

*(Several were originally awarded the Empire Gallantry Medal, which was later replaced by the George Cross.)

Amongst those awarded the George Cross was Sergeant John Beckett who on 28 March 1947 was refuelling a Lancaster at Ein Shemer airfield in the Levant when a fire broke out. He drove the petrol tanker away from the scene, despite it being on fire, until it presented no further danger to his colleagues or the remaining aircraft. He was severely burnt and later died of his injuries.

Another recipient was Corporal Daphne Pearson who on 19 July 1940 approached a crashed and burning aircraft at Detling to rescue the pilot before the fuel tanks and an unexploded bomb inside the aircraft exploded. Pearson protected the pilot from the blast and then entered the burning wreck to check for more of the crew.

The only RAF chaplain to be awarded the George Cross was the Reverend Cecil Pugh, who was killed when his troopship was torpedoed in the Atlantic on 5 July 1941. Pugh remained on board as the ship sank, helping to launch lifeboats and tending to wounded and trapped airmen.

George Medal (GM)

Instituted: 1940

Ribbon: Crimson and blue vertical stripes
Medal: Silver; current monarch on one side with St George
               slaying the dragon on other
Inscription: 'The George Medal'
Level: 2

Introduced at the same time as the George Cross for acts of bravery that were worthy of merit but not quite as outstanding. One of those awarded the GM was Lossiemouth SAR pilot Flight Lieutenant Michael Lakey, whose Sea King rescued 22 survivors from the burning cargo ship *Finneagle* on the night of 2 October 1980. He faced high seas and toxic fumes from the burning cargo and hovered for 1¾ hours to winch all the survivors off the ship. All of Lakey's crew were decorated, including a medical officer who volunteered to take part in the rescue.

Distinguished Service Order (DSO)

Instituted: 1886
Ribbon: Thick crimson vertical stripe flanked by blue
Medal: Silver-gilt cross with crown in centre
Inscription: None
Level: 2

The Distinguished Service Order is awarded to officers who carry out successful command and leadership during active operations. Amongst the DSO's recipients were Group Captain Willie Tait and Air Chief Marshal Basil Embry (who was awarded three bars to add to his DSO) in the Second World War.

Conspicuous Gallantry Cross (CGC)

Instituted: 1993
Ribbon: Red, white and blue stripes
Medal: Silver crown on cross surrounded by wreath
Inscription: None
Level: 2

The CGC replaced the Conspicuous Gallantry Medal (Air) and is awarded for gallantry in operations against the enemy. Squadron Leader Iain MacFarlane was given the CGC in 2005 for his actions in Operation Barras in Sierra Leone.

OTHER MEDALS

Military Cross (MC)
Awarded for actions on land. The first Military Cross to be awarded to a member of the RAF was Corporal David Hayden of the RAF Regiment for his actions in Iraq in rescuing a wounded comrade in 2007.

Distinguished Service Cross (DSC)
The DSC was mainly awarded to navy officers, but some have been awarded to RAF personnel serving on navy ships.

RAF MEDALS
These medals are predominantly awarded to RAF personnel.

Distinguished Flying Cross (DFC)
Instituted: 1918
Ribbon: Diagonal white and purple stripes
Medal: In the centre of the cross, a crown sits above the initials 'RAF', which are set between two wings.
Inscription: None
Level: 3

This gallantry medal was originally awarded only to officers and Warrant Officers but is now for all ranks. In the First World War 1,100 were awarded with over 19,000 awarded in the Second World War. Its related medal, the Distinguished Flying Medal, which was awarded to non-commissioned personnel for bravery in active operations, was discontinued in 1993. A number of DFCs were awarded to Chinook pilots for their actions in Afghanistan.

Air Force Cross (AFC)

Instituted: 1918
Ribbon: Diagonal red and white stripes
Medal: In the centre of a silver cross the figure of Hermes riding a Hawk is depicted.
Inscription: None
Level: 3

Seen as the 'peacetime DFC' the AFC is awarded for exemplary gallantry or devotion to duty on flying duty but not on operations against an enemy. Captain Stanley Cockerell was awarded the AFC for attempting to make the first flight between Cairo and Cape Town in 1920, while Hurricane test pilot George Bulman was a three times awardee. More recently, Squadron Leader 'Disco' Discombe was awarded the AFC in 2015 for safely landing a Battle of Britain Memorial Flight Hurricane after it suffered a major oil leak. In a similar fashion to the fate of the Distinguished Flying Medal, the AFC's companion award for non-commissioned personnel, the Air Force Medal, was discontinued in 1993.

Mention in dispatches (MiD)

A Level 4 award. There is no medal but awardees wear a small brass oak leaf on their tunic. It is awarded for acts of gallantry in active operations.

Queen's Commendation for Bravery in the Air (QCBA)

This Level 4 award is for those acts of bravery while flying but not on combat operations, and those awarded it wear a small silver eagle.

Campaign and service medals

Campaign medals are issued to all eligible armed forces personnel who have served in a recognised conflict. One such is the Burma

Star given to those who took part in the Burma Campaign during the Second World War. Two were only given to RAF personnel: the Aircrew Europe Star and the Clasp to the 1939–45 Star. The Aircrew Europe Star was given to those who had flown operations for at least two months from the start of the war to the D-Day landings. The Clasp was awarded to those fighter aircrew who flew during the Battle of Britain.

More recently the Operational Service Medal Afghanistan, Operational Service Medal Sierra Leone and Operational Service Medal Democratic Republic of Congo were awarded to those who served in those theatres.

There have been three recent individual campaign medals issued for the relevant conflicts – South Atlantic Medal, Gulf Medal and Iraq Medal – and a General Service Medal 2008 was awarded to armed forces personnel who served from 2008 in eastern Africa, western Africa, the Arabian Peninsula, northern Africa and southern Asia.

Royal Air Force Long Service and Good Conduct Medal (LS&GCM)

Awarded to those who have served more than 15 years and whose conduct has reached the highest standard.

Meritorious Service Medal (MSM)

Awarded to a maximum of 60 RAF personnel per year who have displayed the highest standards of unbroken conduct and character.

RAF personnel are also eligible for meritorious service awards such as the CBE, OBE and MBE announced during the Queen's Birthday and New Year's Honours Lists.

CHAPTER THIRTEEN
LIFE IN THE SERVICE

For those in the First World War, service in the RFC was seen as an acceptable way to avoid being in the trenches. While servicing machines overnight in cold and draughty sheds might not have been comfortable, it was preferable to the alternative.

The appeal of the air force in preference to serving in the army or navy has to some extent rested on the location: most RAF postings were to permanent facilities in the form of air bases, which could be close to towns and the associated amenities.

Discipline was also a factor, with those in the army and navy regarding their compatriots in the light blue uniform as being treated more leniently. This would come as a surprise to those subjected to a berating from a Station Warrant Officer who found their dress or haircut unacceptable.

In its first decades, the image of the RAF was different to that of its fellow armed forces. While the army still had to operate on the potentially muddy, wet battlefields and the navy had traditions dating back to Trafalgar, the air force was new and glamorous. For pilots who were part of 'the best flying club in the world', life was a continuation of their school or university days, with the officers' mess the centre of their social world. It was not without its strictures – officers were discouraged from marrying while in their 20s.

During the Second World War, unlike other conflicts the Battle of Britain was fought over the skies of southern England and young fighter pilots were pictured smiling and relaxed before taking to the air. The 'Brylcreem Boys', as RAF personnel were known, were seen as being a bit different.

Post-war newsreels depicted this service of dashing aviators who roared off into the blue in their powerful, silver machines. The appeal of new technology that was always a feature of the RAF was attractive to young men with an interest in engineering or any of the other trades.

RECRUITMENT

Recruitment has depended to an extent on economic and social circumstances. In the years following its formation, air force recruitment was not problematic. As aircraft were not hugely complicated, skill levels required were not unduly high. Unemployment was high and there was the added pull of working in the exciting new world of aviation. There was much less need to recruit following the First World War as the service contracted. When it expanded in the 1930s, it was during a period of mass unemployment.

Men were called up through conscription in the Second World War but thousands volunteered from overseas and from the Commonwealth countries in particular: Canada, Australia, New Zealand, Rhodesia, South Africa and India. A third of RAF personnel were from the Commonwealth.

Following the Second World War recruitment was more difficult, with full employment and skilled men seeing better opportunities elsewhere. There were the added disincentives of constant movement as personnel were posted every two to three years, with the impact that had on children's schooling. In 1950 a new trade structure was brought in to recruit and retain the personnel needed by offering better advancement opportunities. More recently, while there has been a general trend of reducing the size of the service, recruitment has continued when specific trades are required to be maintained.

NATIONAL SERVICE

During the post-war period there was a need for extra personnel to serve in the armed forces and conscription was reintroduced. National Service, introduced in 1947, called up men between the ages of 17 and 21, who were required to serve two years in one of the services. The last of these were demobbed in 1963, by which time almost half a million national servicemen had served in the air force.

PERIOD OF SERVICE

Those who currently enlist sign up for a defined period, which can be extended depending on promotion. After their regular service is over, personnel are required to spend time in the reserves.

Type	Regular service duration (on entry) in years
Officer: short service commission	3–12 (aircrew is 12)
Officer: permanent commission	Until aged 38 or 40 (or after 16 or 18 years' service depending on which date joined) 16–18 (If promoted through the ranks via the internal commissioning scheme)
Non-commissioned aircrew	To age 40 or 18 years in service (whichever was later)
Non-commissioned recruits	9 (Can be extended to 12 or 15 years)

INITIAL TRAINING

For many years a new airman recruit's first taste of life was at RAF Swinderby in the RAF School of Recruit Training. They would receive six weeks of drill, physical exercise, weapons training and field exercises under canvas. The history and values of the RAF were also given. Beginning in the Cold War, instruction on NBC (nuclear, biological, chemical) preventative measures was also carried out.

Recruits would be heavily encouraged by their NCOs to keep their accommodation block neat, tidy and very clean, and standards in the appearance of their personal bedding, clothes and footwear were also expected to be kept high. Any misdemeanour would receive 'jankers' – punishments which had, during the 1950s, included painting coal black and using a toothbrush to paint the lines on the parade ground.

At the end of basic training, a passing-out parade was held with a reviewing officer of senior rank. After a period of leave, the new recruits would move on to the next stage of their training.

Following Swinderby's closure in 1993, recruits are now sent to Halton as part of the Recruit Training Squadron for a 10-week training programme that follows much of the format of the previous basic training given to new airmen and airwomen.

EARLY DISCHARGE

If they find life in uniform is not for them, current non-commissioned recruits have the right to be discharged, as long as they have served 28 days and it is still within the six-month period after enlisting.

≋ MY RAF ≋

R. A. FERGUSON
*Senior Aircraftman, served 1956–59 and Flight
Lieutenant RAFVR(T) 1963–83*

I was called up for national service in 1956 and hated the first few weeks as I felt the NCO's behaviour went a bit far at times. In our hut we had spent hours bulling the floor. Our corporal was not satisfied with our work and he emptied a full coal scuttle all over the floor. He then proceeded to walk all over it, trampling it into the floor! As an ex-Air Cadet, my initial time at Bridgnorth was reduced by two weeks. The last period of my time there was a lot better, with a more understanding officer and NCOs.

I trained as a fighter plotter but, as that trade was being phased out, I became a radar operator. I signed on for an extra year to ensure I got a decent trade and more money. The National Serviceman's pay was paltry compared to what I was earning in civvy street! I reached the rank of Senior Aircraftman but missed out on promotion as I was due to travel home to the UK for two months' annual leave and the unit required a Junior NCO immediately.

Over my service time there were many characters I remember, but two come to mind, both from my time at 751 Signals Unit at Cape Greco in Cyprus. The first was 'Chiefy' Burns; he was responsible for the overall running of the technical site. He never seemed to get upset about any problem and always looked after his airmen. He was a real father figure to those in the unit. The other was our commanding officer Squadron Leader MacDonald, always immaculate in his dress, desert boots and a fly swat. He was very rarely seen in the tented lines and seemed uninterested in the well-being of the unit. When going 'off camp' he mostly carried a Bren gun and a side arm, earning him the nickname of 'Bren Gun Bertie'.

The best aspect of my time in uniform was the friendships that developed, especially at Cape Greco. As we were all living under the same conditions you had to learn to get on with the conditions and the blokes around you. It has often been said that you went into the services as a boy and came out as a man. I think that is very true. As one becomes older you remember the good times like the travel, the parties and so on. The bad times during the EOKA Emergency tend to be forgotten. My abiding memory of my time is that by the end of it I knew a lot more about what I was capable of and what made me the person I am.

PROMOTION

Promotion can be achieved in two ways: substantive or acting. Acting may be paid or unpaid and does not guarantee subsequent promotion to that rank. Substantive promotion is achieved through approval by a commanding officer on the basis of time and qualification. For example, a Leading Aircraftman or Leading Aircraftwoman wishing to gain promotion to the rank above would need to pass a test (Trade Ability Test (TAT) No. 1), and would need to have completed a year's satisfactory service. Selection boards sit to consider promotion to ranks of Corporal and above.

For officers, promotion can depend on several factors such as merit, which branch they are in and their time in the service. Selection boards sit annually to consider candidates for promotion. There are additional qualifications for some ranks. Squadron Leaders wishing to become Wing Commanders have to complete an eight-week Intermediate Command and Staff Course (Air).

OVERSEAS

As with any of the armed forces, a recruit might join in order to 'see the world', and the RAF began life during the First World War with most of its personnel deployed overseas.

With the end of the Empire and the Cold War, and financial restrictions, the reduction in permanent bases overseas has limited the possibilities available for the current recruit. But over the past century, RAF personnel have been based in all of these countries or territories:

Aden	Germany	Norway
Afghanistan	Ghana	Oman
Algeria	Gibraltar	Palestine
Australia	Greece	Russia
Austria	Hong Kong	Sardinia
Azores	Iceland	Saudi Arabia
Belgium	India	Sicily
Belize	Iraq	Sierra Leone
Borneo	Israel	Singapore
Burma	Italy	Somalia
Canada	Jordan	Sudan
Ceylon	Kenya	Tanganyika
Corsica	Libya	Thailand
Crete	Macedonia	Turkey
Cyprus	Malaya	United Arab Emirates
Egypt	Maldives	Vietnam
Eritrea	Malta	Yugoslavia
Falkland Islands	Morocco	
Faroe Islands	Netherlands	
France	Nigeria	

> ### RAF TRADITIONS
>
> **Time**
>
> It is a tradition that no matter the location, 'Zulu' time (GMT) is used in order to prevent any errors through misunderstanding of local time zones.

MESSING

Amongst the facilities on any station are the different messes. (The word's usage goes back to the medieval era when it was used to describe foodstuffs collected for a marching army.)

There are three different messes on a station:

▶ Officers' mess

▶ Warrant Officers' and Sergeants' mess

▶ Junior ranks' mess (all other ranks).

Officers' mess

The officers' mess is the social centre for officers on a station and provides accommodation for single officers. Every officer on a station is automatically a member of the mess.

The concept was based on the traditions and customs used by the army and the navy. Dress codes are stipulated and different levels can be indicated for specific times, from smart/casual (polo shirts and jeans) to the mess dress uniforms for formal events. Clothes that are unacceptable at any time include T-shirts, hoodies and flip-flops.

A regular feature is 'Happy Hour', normally held on a Friday, which is not limited to being 60 minutes long. Formal events are dining-in and guest nights. Attendees follow strict rules laid down for dress and the structure of the event. For example, it is considered bad etiquette to leave the dining room to visit the toilet during the meal.

Conversations are expected to exclude religion, politics or 'shop', i.e. talking about work. At the end of the meal the Loyal Toast is made to the Queen. One of the most well-known of RAF customs is that the decanters carrying the port and Madeira for the toast must not be passed to the right, nor should they touch the table.

DID YOU KNOW?

The expression 'backhander' originates from when an empty glass that has been missed is passed to the left to catch up the decanter. When it is filled, it is then handed back to the right to reach its owner.

While a place of formality, the officer's mess can also be where hair is firmly let down and steam is let off once dinner has ended.

Cars could be moved so that they were stuck between trees, or carried (or driven) into the building itself. Pyrotechnics or smoke bombs could be set to go off at opportune moments during speeches. One event saw a model Buccaneer fire mini rockets over the heads of those dining and into the mess walls.

Various games or sports have been played. They include:

Deck landings	Participants would be launched towards the dinner tables, on which they would slide along, if the surface was liberally lubricated with beer.
Fireball hockey	A 'ball' made of flammable material would be set alight before the game began. Goalkeepers were advised to wear oven gloves.

Potholing	This saw the participant crawling under the dinner tables to tie a fellow officer's or guest's shoelaces together.
Mess rugby	Two teams played rugby inside using anything but a rugby ball.
Jousting	Riding bicycles, participants would use domestic mops to unseat their opponent.
Highcockalorum	Participants would jump onto the backs of their teammates, and the highest pile was the winner.
Spinning	Teams race to drink beer, spin around a broomstick then return to the starting point.
Crud	At a snooker table, two teams attempt to sink the other's ball.
Piano burning	As stated. The custom of pianos being burnt is said to go back to the First World War as a mark of respect to those flyers who had died.
Ceiling walking	Boots would be dipped in black paint and then the wearer would 'walk' the ceiling.

Warrant Officers' and Sergeants' mess

The Warrant Officers' and Sergeants' mess provides the same facilities and events as for the commissioned officers.

Junior ranks' mess

These messes are predominantly to provide dining arrangements for airmen and airwomen. In 1970 single men were offered the option of staying off base, following a change in regulations. Accommodation was previously provided for free but this change came with an increase in pay.

NAAFI

No account of the RAF can exclude a mention of the NAAFI (Navy, Army and Air Force Institute), which has been providing servicemen and women with goods and services since 1921. It runs recreation facilities and canteens, many of them mobile, both at home and overseas. It also sells goods: during the Second World War 24 million cigarettes were sold each day. The same war saw the institution reach a peak of 110,000 NAAFI employees, 4,000 of them artists providing an entertainment service. The NAAFI continues to operate in the UK and at locations in the Falklands, Gibraltar and Germany.

RAF TRADITIONS:

Drinking:

As alcohol has helped encourage social bonds between squadron members during beer-calls or other occasions, a number of drinking traditions have been established. 1(F) Sqn had a drinking game called the Wharton Handicap in which teams raced around the pubs of Stamford, near to their base at Wittering. It was named after a certain squadron pilot's stag night. The Harrier OCU had a tradition that after a pilot had completed their first hover they had to drink from a large tankard, suitably named the 'Hover Pot'. Squadrons have even had their own drinks: 43 Sqn, known as the Fighting Cocks, have a 'Fighting Cocktail' made up of Kahlúa and Baileys, to mimic the black and white chequerboard markings used on their aircraft.

DISCIPLINE

'Discipline is to be taught and maintained on its true basis and not on that of fear of punishment.'
SECTION 998, QUEEN'S REGULATIONS

As with all armed forces, discipline is a necessity, although its nature has changed through the years. In the 1930s boy apprentices could be given the lash for offences such as stealing. Discipline is outlined in the Queen's Regulations or Station Standing Orders, and personnel can be subjected to a range of actions. An individual can be given extra duties, a formal interview, returned to unit or, more seriously, given a formal warning and made the subject of an administrative report. Other sanctions are available depending on the severity of the offence, and personnel can find themselves suspended from duty, forfeiting pay, being reduced in rank, remustered to another trade or posted elsewhere. They can also be discharged. As well as these actions, officers face having their commission terminated, being removed from branch or having time promotions delayed. Summary punishments include forfeiture of seniority, fines, reprimand, restriction of privileges, being confined to camp or paying compensation (up to £1,000). Court martials are held for serious offences and, if custodial sentences are issued, the individual is sent to the Military Corrective Training Centre (MCTC) in Colchester.

ASSOCIATIONS AND REUNIONS

Many former personnel meet up with ex-colleagues, in formal or informal meetings, to continue the friendships made while in uniform. Amongst those are the 'Old Haltonians' – the RAF Halton Apprentices Association. Another is that of the 751 Signals Unit based at Cape Greco in Cyprus during the 1950s, which meets on an annual basis.

Some of the associations include:

- ▶ 100 Group Association

- ▶ 3(F) Squadron Association

- ▶ Administrative Apprentices Association

- ▶ Air Loadmaster Association

- ▶ Bomber Command Association

- ▶ Coastal Command and Maritime Air Association

- ▶ National Service (RAF) Association

- ▶ RAF Binbrook Signals Squadron Association

- ▶ RAF Locking Apprentices Association

- ▶ RAF Regiment Association.

DID YOU KNOW?

The RAF has its own private club. The RAF Club was formed in 1918 and membership is open to current or former officers. The club's property in Piccadilly in London includes a ballroom, a tavern, library, dining room and bedrooms.

THOSE WHO SERVED

Many well-known people have served in the RAF, including:

- ▶ Alan Bates (actor)

- ▶ Alec Bedser (cricketer)

- ▶ Arthur C. Clarke (science-fiction writer)

- ▶ Bill Shankly (football manager)

- ▶ Bill Wyman (rock musician)

- ▶ Billy Liddell (footballer)

- ▶ Bob Monkhouse (comedian)

- ▶ Bruce Forsyth (entertainer)

- ▶ Christopher Lee (actor)
- ▶ Dan Maskell (tennis commentator)
- ▶ David Bailey (photographer)
- ▶ David Tomlinson (actor)
- ▶ Denholm Elliot (actor)
- ▶ Des O'Connor (entertainer)
- ▶ Dirk Bogarde (actor)
- ▶ Donald Pleasence (actor)
- ▶ Eric Sykes (comedian/writer)
- ▶ Fred Trueman (cricketer)
- ▶ George Chisholm (musician)
- ▶ Henry Cotton (golfer)
- ▶ James Hadley Chase (writer)
- ▶ Jimmy Edwards (actor)
- ▶ John Cobb (speed record holder)
- ▶ Ken Adam (film production designer)
- ▶ Ken Loach (film director)
- ▶ Kenneth Wolstenholme (commentator)
- ▶ Leo Baxendale (cartoonist)
- ▶ Max Bygraves (entertainer)
- ▶ Michael Bentine (comedian)
- ▶ Nicholas Winton (humanitarian)
- ▶ Norman Tebbit (politician)

- ▶ Pam Ayres (poet)
- ▶ Patrick Moore (astronomer)
- ▶ Peter Sellers (actor)
- ▶ Raymond Baxter (TV presenter)
- ▶ Rex Harrison (actor)
- ▶ Rex Hunt (governor)
- ▶ Richard Attenborough (actor/film director)
- ▶ Richard Burton (actor)
- ▶ Roald Dahl (writer)
- ▶ Robert Hardy (actor)
- ▶ Ronnie Corbett (comedian)
- ▶ Roy Hudd (actor/comedian)
- ▶ Steve Race (musician/broadcaster)
- ▶ T. E. Lawrence (soldier)
- ▶ Ted Croker (football administrator)
- ▶ Terence Rattigan (playwright)
- ▶ Tony Benn (politician)
- ▶ Tony Hancock (comedian)
- ▶ Warren Mitchell (actor)
- ▶ W. E. Johns (writer)
- ▶ William Wales (helicopter pilot).

PART 4

THE TECHNOLOGY

CHAPTER FOURTEEN
THE AIRCRAFT

A repeating pattern can be seen with the twentieth century's two main conflicts, when the RAF rapidly expanded during wartime and then contracted at the end of the conflict, before continuing with its wartime aircraft for longer than envisaged in peacetime. For example, First World War DH.9As were flown into the 1930s and the last Bristol Beaufighter sortie was flown in 1960.

In the Korean War it was clear that swept-wing fighters were now required. The straight-wing Gloster Meteors flown by the RAAF were no match for the MiG 17s, and given that similar British-built machines were as yet unavailable, over 400 F-86 Sabres were procured from America. The heavy bomber force was still operating propeller-driven types such as Lincolns (a development of the Lancaster) and another US-supplied acquisition, the Washington – the British version of the B-29 Superfortress.

The mid-1950s finally saw the RAF established with a new generation of jet machines: swept-wing fighters in the shape of the Supermarine Swift and the Hawker Hunter and a quantum leap in the bomber force with the three V-bombers: the four-engined Valiant, Victor and Vulcan. The Canberra, which had been introduced in 1951, was also in service as a light bomber.

A blow, to the RAF came in the shape of the 1957 Defence White Paper which proposed a reduction in the strength of conventional forces, with the emphasis to be on nuclear deterrence. Home defence would eventually be achieved through the deployment of surface-to-air missiles rather than manned fighters, and in 1956 Chancellor of the Exchequer Harold Macmillan had even suggested abolishing Fighter Command completely – although one aircraft that did escape cancellation was the English Electric Lightning, capable of Mach 2 speeds.

In the 1960s, the RAF suffered again when three UK-designed projects were cancelled. The TSR.2 low-level bomber/reconnaissance aircraft, the P.1154 supersonic V/STOL fighter and the HS.681 jet transport were all abandoned, though their replacements proved to be highly capable aircraft: the Blackburn Buccaneer, the US-built F-4 Phantom and Lockheed C-130 Hercules respectively.

Despite these political setbacks, during the 1960s the British aircraft industry supplied much of the RAF's inventory. The revolutionary Hawker Siddeley Harrier entered squadron service. In the maritime role the Shackletons were replaced by the advanced Nimrod, a derivative of the de Havilland Comet, the world's first jetliner. Long-range transport aircraft such as the VC10 and Belfast were also brought into service.

The RAF's strength was reduced in the 1970s to around 750 front-line aircraft. The emphasis was now on the North Atlantic Treaty Organisation (NATO), and to that end a large contingent of aircraft was based in Germany. One of these was the Anglo-French Sepecat Jaguar in the low-level ground attack and reconnaissance roles. This was later replaced in some squadrons by another aircraft built as an international collaboration. The Panavia Tornado, a joint British, German and Italian venture, entered squadron service at the start of the 1980s. A fighter version was also produced, which replaced the Lightning and the Phantom, and this in turn was later replaced by the Typhoon as the sole air defence fighter.

CURRENT AIRCRAFT

These aircraft make up the current inventory:

COMBAT
Panavia Tornado GR.4
Maximum speed: Mach 1.3
Maximum altitude: 50,000 ft
Armament: Brimstone, Storm Shadow, Paveway II, Paveway III, Paveway IV, 1 x Mauser 27 mm cannon, Sidewinder AAM
Crew: 2

The Tornado first flew in 1974 and entered squadron service with 9 Sqn in 1982. It is the only swing-wing aircraft to have been part of the RAF's inventory. It fitted the air force's requirements for a day/night, low-level strike/reconnaissance aircraft, and the GR.1 version was part of the nuclear strike force until the 1990s. The GR.1A version was designed for the tactical reconnaissance role and the GR.1B carried Sea Eagle anti-shipping missiles.

A major upgrade resulted in the GR.4 version, which featured enhanced avionics and the introduction of night vision goggles. Tornadoes have seen combat action in Kosovo, Iraq, Afghanistan, Libya and Syria. The aircraft replaced the Harrier in the close air support mission in Afghanistan in 2009, where it carried out 'show of force' sorties, day and night, by flying fast (500 mph) and low (100 ft) over enemy positions, without using weapons.

Tornadoes are based at Marham in Norfolk and will be retired in 2019, to be replaced by the F-35.

DID YOU KNOW?

In 1999 RAF Tornadoes from Brüggen in Germany, taking part in operations over Kosovo, flew missions lasting seven hours.

Eurofighter Typhoon FGR.4

Maximum speed:	Mach 2
Maximum altitude:	65,000 ft
Armament:	1 x 27 mm Mauser cannon, AIM-120 AMRAAM, AIM-132 ASRAAM, Enhanced Paveway II, Paveway IV
Crew:	1

Entering service in 2003, Typhoons are now based at three stations: Lossiemouth and Coningsby in the UK and Mount Pleasant in the Falkland Islands. They are tasked with 24/7 quick reaction alert (QRA) duties. They can be scrambled to intercept any unknown aircraft that requires airborne verification, and, if required, can be authorised for overland supersonic flight.

They are described as 'swing-role' – able to change quickly from one role to another, be it interception to ground attack, without landing to change payload. Typhoons saw their first combat action over Libya in 2011 and dropped Paveway IV precision-guided bombs on Iraq and Syria.

Lockheed Martin F-35B

Maximum speed:	Mach 1.6
Maximum altitude:	50,000 ft
Armament:	AIM-120 AMRAAM, AIM-132 ASRAAM, Paveway IV
Crew:	1

The F-35 is a fifth-generation stealth combat aircraft that first flew in December 2006. Its advanced sensors and stealth technology are coupled with a short take-off and vertical landing (STOVL) capability. F-35Bs will operate from the next generation of navy carriers as well as airfields.

The F-35B pilot has no head-up display, as all the information is presented on head-down displays or on the pilot's helmet visor. Sensors around the fuselage allow a 360-degree field of view 'through the aircraft', offering unprecedented situational awareness.

617 Sqn at Marham will be the first operational unit in British service, its commanding officer drawn alternately from the RAF and the navy.

The F-35B is designed to perform intelligence, surveillance, reconnaissance, air-to-ground, air-to-air and electronic attack missions. It is intended to be equipped with the SPEAR 3 (selective precision effects at range) missile.

INTELLIGENCE, SURVEILLANCE, TARGET ACQUISITION AND RECONNAISSANCE (ISTAR)

Reconnaissance has always played a vital part in the RAF's ability to deploy weapon-bearing aircraft effectively, and the latest technology offers a greater range of capabilities than ever before. The current range of aircraft is grouped under the ISTAR category.

Boeing E-3D Sentry AEW.1

Maximum speed: 530 mph
Maximum altitude: 35,000 ft
Armament: None
Crew: 4 flight crew, 14 technicians and mission specialists

The Sentry performs the airborne surveillance and command and control roles. The radar antenna is mounted above the fuselage in a 30-ft-diameter disc which rotates at 6 rpm. At altitude it has a range of 350 miles.

A team of onboard mission specialists interpret the incoming data, which is then passed on to the appropriate aerial assets through voice communication or secure datalink.

Boeing RC-135W Rivet Joint
Maximum speed: 550 mph
Maximum altitude: 50,000 ft
Armament: None
Crew: 3 flight crew, up to 25 mission specialists

Rivet Joints are used to gather signals intelligence (SIGINT), which is then disseminated via various communication methods. Three Rivet Joint aircraft were bought to replace the Nimrod R.1.

Raytheon Sentinel R.1
Maximum speed: 600 mph
Maximum altitude: 40,000 ft
Armament: None
Crew: 5

The Sentinel is a ground surveillance aircraft based on the Bombardier Global Express business jet. It has been used to support military action in Iraq, Afghanistan and Libya, with a focus on countering improvised explosive devices (IEDs) and monitoring suspicious vehicles. It has also been utilised in civilian scenarios, such as the flooding in south-east England in 2014, where its radar was used to monitor river levels.

Sentinel was to be withdrawn in 2015 following the 2010 Strategic Defence and Security Review (SDSR), but was retained in service following its performance in Afghanistan and Libya.

Beechcraft Shadow R.1
Maximum speed: 350 mph
Maximum altitude: 35,000 ft
Armament: None

Crew: 5/7

Little has been released about the equipment fitted in the Shadow, which is a converted Beechcraft King Air 350CER.

General Atomics MQ-9A Reaper
Maximum speed: 287 mph
Maximum altitude: 50,000 ft
Armament: Paveway II, AGM-114 Hellfire missiles
Crew: 0

Deployed to Afghanistan in 2007 the Reaper is the first remotely piloted air system (RPAS) to see front-line service with the RAF. This 'drone' is employed in the intelligence, surveillance and reconnaissance (ISR) role, where its long endurance and sensor suite (infrared, electro-optical, image-intensified TV, synthetic aperture radar and ground moving target indicator) allows it to remain on station and continue surveillance long after its manned counterparts have had to return to base. Reapers are flown during most of their operations by pilots thousands of miles away.

TRANSPORT, TANKER AND COMMUNICATIONS

Boeing C-17 Globemaster III
Maximum speed: 520 mph
Maximum altitude: 45,000 ft
Armament: None
Crew: 3

The US-built C-17 is a strategic transporter capable of carrying a 74-ton load, which can mean 13 Land Rovers or three Apache attack helicopters. It can operate out of airfields with a 3,500 ft runway and its four jet engines can provide enough reverse thrust to taxi the aircraft up a two-degree incline. Globemasters can be equipped for casevac operations.

Airbus A330 Voyager K.2/K.3

Maximum speed: 567 mph
Maximum altitude: 41,000 ft
Armament: None
Crew: Up to 11

The Voyager is a conversion based on the Airbus A330-200 airliner. It is equipped for the long-range air transport and aerial refuelling tanker roles. The K.2 version has two refuelling points under each wing while the K.3 has the same with an additional point under the fuselage. Unlike other tanker conversions the Voyager had no extra fuel tanks installed and so the full cabin capacity is available for personnel. The Voyagers are operated under a private finance initiative, whereby the private consortium AirTanker own and maintain the aircraft.

Lockheed C-130J Hercules

Maximum speed: 368 mph
Maximum altitude: 40,000 ft
Armament: None
Crew: 3

The Hercules is a tactical air transporter and in RAF service has operated in many parts of the world. Amongst many other operations, they have taken part in famine relief air drops in western Nepal in 1973; evacuated Britons from Iran in January 1979; formed part of the Ceasefire Monitoring Force in Rhodesia in December 1979; transported food supplies to Ethiopia in 1985; and delivered aid to the Philippines in 2013 after Typhoon Haiyan. One of the most unusual flights was to parachute-drop Royal Marines into the Atlantic to board the QE2 following a bomb scare on the liner.

DID YOU KNOW?

The Hercules was the first RAF aircraft to be deployed in the Falklands conflict when four were sent to form the air bridge to Ascension Island. Hercules were used on long-range missions to drop supplies and personnel to the task force in the South Atlantic.

Airbus A400M Atlas

Maximum speed: 470 mph
Maximum altitude: 40,000 ft
Armament: None
Crew: 3

This planned replacement for the C-130 entered service in 2014. The turboprop Atlas was the product of a six-nation collaboration and operates as both a tactical and strategic transporter. The Atlas offers greater cargo capacity and range than Lockheed's legendary workhouse. It can carry 108 paratroops or 36 tons of cargo.

BAE Systems 146

Maximum speed: 495 mph
Maximum altitude: 31,000 ft
Armament: None
Crew: 5

Developed from the successful four-engined airliner, the CC.2 version is used for VIP transport while the C.3 is fitted with a rear cargo door and is capable of carrying 10 tons of freight. It can also carry 94 passengers.

TRAINING

BAE Systems Hawk T.1

Maximum speed: 633 mph
Maximum altitude: 48,000 ft
Armament: 1,000 lb of ordnance, including 30 mm cannon
                  and Sidewinder
Crew: 1 x pupil, 1 x instructor

The Hawk's progress into service was unusual in that no prototype was built. The first Hawk to take to the air, in August 1974, was XX154 and came straight off the production line.

The Hawk was used as the advanced jet trainer to train pilots in how to fly fast jets and then how to fly in combat. It replaced the Folland Gnat and Hawker Hunter. The Red Arrows were equipped with Hawk T.1s in 1979 and they are also flown by 100 Sqn.

BAE Systems Hawk T.2

Maximum speed: 640 mph
Maximum altitude: 42,000 ft
Armament: Various
Crew: 1 x pupil, 1 x instructor

The Hawk T.2 entered service in 2008. It provides students with the avionics and electronic cockpit displays they will encounter after their progression to front-line aircraft. For example interceptions can be simulated by synthetic radar information being sent to the displays in the cockpit via a datalink.

Beechcraft King Air B200

Maximum speed: 300 mph
Maximum altitude: 28,000 ft
Armament: None
Crew: 2

The King Air is a twin-engine turboprop used to train aircrew in flying multi-engined aircraft in both basic and advanced phases. It is after their period on the King Air that pilots are awarded their wings.

Short Tucano T.1

Maximum speed: 345 mph
Maximum altitude: 25,000 ft
Armament: None
Crew: 2

Despite being a turboprop, the Tucano T.1 provides basic fast-jet training to air force and navy pilots. It is used to teach aircraft handling, low-level and formation flying.

Grob Tutor T.1

Maximum speed: 210 mph
Maximum altitude: 10,000 ft
Armament: None
Crew: 2

The Tutor is used for elementary flying training and also by University Air Squadrons and Air Cadet Air Experience Flights.

Vigilant T.1

Maximum speed: 150 mph
Maximum altitude: 8,000 ft
Armament: None
Crew: 2

The Vigilant is the name given to the Grob 109B powered glider, which is used for giving basic flying training to air cadets.

Viking T.1

Maximum speed: 137 mph
Maximum altitude: 8,000 ft

Armament: None
Crew: 2

The Viking is the glider used by air cadets for training and it is in this aircraft that many make their first solo flights.

HELICOPTERS

Boeing Chinook
Maximum speed: 185 mph
Maximum altitude: 15,000 ft
Armament: M134 Minigun and M60D machine gun
Crew: 4

The Chinook is the RAF's heavy-lift helicopter. It can carry 55 troops, or 10 tons of freight, and has been heavily used in recent conflict areas in Afghanistan and Iraq. It was noted for its ability to operate in the emergency casevac role.

DID YOU KNOW?

In Afghanistan in 2010, Chinooks transported 96,000 passengers.

Aérospatiale Puma HC.2
Maximum speed: 192 mph
Maximum altitude: 19,700 ft
Armament: Can be fitted with 2 x general purpose machine
                  guns
Crew: 2

The Puma HC.2 version is an upgraded version of the HC.1, which was brought into service in 1971. HC.2s have more range and more powerful engines than HC.1s, as well as upgraded defensive aids. This battlefield support helicopter is able to be carried by the C-17.

Griffin HAR.2

Maximum speed: 161 mph
Maximum altitude: 20,000 ft
Armament: None
Crew: 4 (in SAR role)

As well as for training, the Griffin is used by 84 Sqn in Cyprus in the search and rescue role, where it can be equipped with the Bambi Bucket water-dropping system for firefighting.

AgustaWestland AW109 Grand New

Maximum speed: 193 mph
Maximum altitude: 10,000 ft
Armament: None
Crew: 1

The AW109 is used in the command support air transport (CSAT) role by 32 (The Royal) Sqn. It carries high-ranking military officers and government ministers as well as high-value cargo items.

Eurocopter Squirrel HT.1

Maximum speed: 178 mph
Maximum altitude: 16,000 ft
Armament: None
Crew: 2

The Squirrel is a single-engined helicopter used in both the basic and advanced trainer roles. It replaced the Gazelle in 1997.

CHAPTER FIFTEEN

ENGINES, WEAPONS AND EQUIPMENT

In its 100-year history the RAF has seen advancements in all aspects of its operational equipment. Much of what is used nowadays would have been unimaginable to those early airmen.

ENGINES

The revolution in transportation that the Wright brothers began in 1903 saw power plants able to propel a passenger for a sustained distance through the air. Their self-built engine produced 12 hp.

Various layouts of fuselage, wings and control surfaces were trialled until by the 1910s aircraft were generally biplanes with either a 'pusher' engine at the rear of the fuselage or a 'tractor' type with the engine and propeller at the very front. One of the mainstays of the RFC was the tractor BE.2c, which flew with a Royal Aircraft Factory No. 1 engine, producing 92 hp. One of the finest RFC fighters, the Sopwith Camel, was powered by an engine in the 130–150 hp output range. It was of the rotary type, in that the crankcase and cylinders rotated around a stationary crankshaft. Rotary engines were effective in their time but because of their width caused excessive drag, and by the 1920s they were regarded as obsolete.

Inline engines, either straight or V-layout, took over as the standard type of piston engine. Engines, as with the airframe and other aspects of aircraft design, have developed rapidly through the years, and by the 1930s the Rolls-Royce Kestrel that powered the Hawker Hart was capable of producing 685 hp.

The dominant British engine of the Second World War was the Rolls-Royce Merlin, used in the Spitfire, Hurricane, Mosquito and Lancaster. The Merlin II at the start of the war produced 1,030 hp. The need in wartime to be ahead of the enemy aircraft's capabilities meant that development was constant, and three years later the Merlin IX was producing almost a quarter more power. Later mark Spitfires were powered by 2,050 hp Griffons, and in 1945 the ultimate in piston-engined fighter aircraft used by the air force, the Hawker Tempest II, entered service with its 2,526 hp Bristol Centaurus. The piston engine had seen a steady improvement in power in the four decades since first used, but the next stage in aircraft engines was to see another leap forward.

Jet engines

On 15 May 1941 a small aircraft took to the air at Cranwell. It was a Gloster E.28/39, the UK's first jet aircraft, and it ushered in a new era in military aviation. Its engine, the Power Jets W.1, was designed by serving officer Frank Whittle and produced 850 lb of jet thrust. Whittle's turbojet was followed by the engine that powered the only Allied jet to fly during the war: the Gloster Meteor. The Mark I Meteor had two Rolls-Royce Wellands, each producing 1,700 lb of thrust. As with piston engines, power output was not long in being increased.

In 1945, a Meteor set a new world record of 606 mph with the 3,500 lb thrust of the Derwent V. The Derwent V was a scaled-down version of the Nene, the engine given to the Soviet Union in 1946 by the British government, which formed the basis of the power plant of the MiG 15 used against British and American aircraft in the Korean War. The Nene was the most powerful turbojet engine at the time.

GREAT MEN OF THE AIR FORCE
SIR FRANK WHITTLE

Whittle was an apprentice at Cranwell in 1923 but was soon selected for officer training. In his end-of-course thesis, 'Future Developments in Aircraft Design', he wrote of the need for aircraft to fly high and fast – at speeds up to 500 mph – for which they would require new types of engine.

While an instructor at the Central Flying School he developed his ideas for a gas turbine engine that would power an aircraft without turning a propeller. He patented his idea in 1930, but it was not picked up by industry or the RAF.

In 1936 he received the financial backing for his turbojet idea, and a company was formed called Power Jets Ltd. Whittle's engine designs were developed into the Rolls-Royce Welland and Derwent power plants which were used in the Gloster Meteor.

Whittle's Power Jets company was nationalised in 1944, and he retired from the air force in 1948, at the rank of Air Commodore. Following his death in 1996 his ashes were interred at Cranwell, carried there in a Meteor jet flown in formation with a Vampire piloted by his son Ian.

Axial-flow

By the end of the 1950s the first generation of jet fighters such as the Meteor and MiG 15 were being replaced. The new types were the products of new design thinking and engine development. Axial-flow engines, more efficient and producing more thrust than the early centrifugal compressor type of jet engines, were now being designed.

One of the aircraft to be brought into service with this new type of engine was the Hawker Hunter in 1954. It was powered by a single Rolls-Royce Avon, which produced 6,500 lb of thrust. This highly successful engine was also used in the Comet airliner and Canberra bomber.

The Avon was also used in a new generation of fighter for the RAF: the English Electric Lightning. Unlike the Hunter's Avons the

Lightning's had reheat – the injection of fuel into the hot exhaust to produce extra thrust; when this extra power was applied, it gave later Mark 6 Lightnings a combined amount of 32,720 lb of thrust. With its twin Avons, the Lightning's rate of climb was an initial 50,000 ft per minute, and it could also reach Mach 2.

Turbofans

Turbofans were a later engine development that brought greater efficiency by allowing air to bypass the combustion stage. They used a large fan at the front of the engine and an additional turbine at the rear.

One of the most innovative turbofans was the Rolls-Royce Pegasus. The direction of its engine thrust could be varied, through directionally controlled nozzles. Air was also diverted to reaction control jets on the wing and fuselage to provide control when normal flying surfaces were inoperable in the hover. The Pegasus was only used in the Harrier. The first version, from 1960, produced 9,000 lb of thrust while the later 107 version used in the GR.9 produced 23,800 lb.

The RAF's current fast jets are powered by turbofans. The Tornado has two RB199s (9,100 lb of thrust to 16,400 lb of thrust with reheat each) and the Typhoon has two Eurojet EJ200s (13,500 lb of thrust to 20,230 lb with reheat each).

The RAF's newest combat aircraft, the F-35B, requires a large amount of thrust due to its STOVL capabilities. Its single Pratt & Whitney F135-PW-600, when combined with the forward lift fan, produces 40,650 lb of thrust when in the hover.

PHOTOGRAPHIC RECONNAISSANCE (PR)

Cameras came into their own during the First World War. Images were captured on 5 x 4-inch glass plates, and the bulky cameras were initially handheld over the side before being fixed to the fuselage. Trench maps were produced and a new trade of photo interpreter was created to provide analysis.

As ground defences increased, PR aircraft were forced to fly higher, necessitating cameras with greater focal length – the British 'L' type could be fitted with a 20-inch lens. Roll film had been introduced during the war, and in the 1920s the 5 x 5 inch F24 camera took 125 exposures on its spool.

However, aerial photography skills were lost after the First World War and it wasn't until the 1930s that thoughts turned again to how to provide this vital service. Australian Sidney Cotton was employed to fly his civilian Lockheed 12A equipped with cameras on clandestine missions over Germany up to the beginning of the Second World War. 'Cotton's Circus' began with his Lockheed and two unarmed Spitfires, which flew the typical strategic reconnaissance mission profile of high altitude (25–35,000 ft while remaining below the tell-tale contrail height) and high speed (the PR Spitfires reached speeds 30 mph faster than normal service versions) in order to outrun any intercepting fighters. In 1940 the Circus became No. 1 Photographic Reconnaissance Unit (PRU).

The photographs required analysing, and to that end the Central Interpretation Unit at Medmenham carried out photographic interpretation. One innovation of the time was the use of stereoscopic viewing: by having two cameras taking overlapping images of the same location, a '3D' image could be viewed through a special viewer. It aided interpreters in noticing features and evaluating the height of objects.

The unit made many significant contributions to the war effort through individual discoveries or the monitoring of ongoing situations, resulting in crucial intelligence gained on the following German sites and targets:

- Invasion barges, 1940
- U-boat production, 1941
- *Bismarck* and *Prinz Eugen*, 1941
- Bruneval radar site, 1941

▶ *Tirpitz*, 1942

▶ Messerschmitt Me 163 rocket fighter, 1943

▶ V1 flying bomb, 1943

▶ V2 ballistic missile, 1943.

Cameras

The F24 camera was still used during the war, but the main camera was the F8, which could be fitted with a 250-exposure film magazine and a 40-inch lens for high-altitude work. Its 7 x 7-inch format allowed better details to be recorded than with the F24's 5 x 5-inch format.

The F52 camera was the first to be designed during the war and became the standard model. It was an enlarged development of the F24 and took 8½ x 7-inch size images with lenses up to 40-inch focal length and with a 500-exposure magazine.

The last RAF aircraft to carry 'wet' film cameras was the Canberra PR.9. It was upgraded with a rapid deployment electro-optical system (RADEOS) as used by the American U-2. It could send its 'real-time' high-resolution imagery through a datalink to the ground. Its capability was shown when an image of London taken at 47,000 ft, from over 80 miles away while over the Isle of Wight, showed the time on Big Ben's clock face. The Canberra was retired in 2006.

The dedicated tactical reconnaissance Tornado GR.1A version had in-built infrared sensors more sensitive than conventional optical ones. They could detect where an aircraft had moved away from its position on an airfield. It was also equipped with a long-range RAPTOR (Reconnaissance Airborne Pod Tornado) pod. Its electro-optical and infrared images could be viewed in the cockpit or directly by ground-based interpreters while in flight.

≋ MY RAF ⊯

KEVIN HOWES
Corporal, served 1980–95

I was 24 years old when I joined the RAF, having worked in shops since leaving school aged 16. I felt I wasn't being pushed enough whilst working in shops so wanted something to stretch me a bit. I joined in December 1980, doing my six-week basic training at RAF Swinderby. This was hard, especially all the cleaning of kit and the drill, etc., but it was also very enjoyable and certainly made you work as a team. It gave you a great deal of discipline.

I joined Trade Group 14, the photographic trade. It had two areas: Ground Photography section, which did all the camera shots of parades, portraits, anything you would do normally with a camera; and Air Photography section, which processed film taken by aircraft, producing prints from the negatives. These could be anything from 9 x 9 inch up to 40 x 40 inch in size! I joined the latter section after I was invited to go along to the Joint School of Photography (JSOP) at RAF Cosford and liked what I saw.

After basic training I went to RAF St Mawgan in Cornwall as part of the Station Warrant Officer's working party, as my trade training course at JSOP was not due to start for a few weeks. It was there that I forged a friendship with a Geordie called Steve Tindale. We travelled down on the train from Swinderby to Newquay, a journey of 11 hours. All the way down he was talking to me and all I kept saying was 'yes' or 'no' as

I couldn't understand a word he was saying! But over the next few weeks I learnt Geordie off to a tee. We are still in contact to this day, over 30 years later.

We were on Air Photographic Processor 2 course number 16 and did around 16 weeks' trade training where we learnt to process films – everything from 16 mm cine film to rolls of 9-inch film hundreds of feet long. Having completed the course, I ended up at the Joint Air Reconnaissance Intelligence Centre (JARIC) at RAF Brampton in Cambridgeshire, reaching the rank of Corporal after just over three years.

During my time at JARIC I did two tours of Northern Ireland, where the job involved film processing and printing as at JARIC. This was the most rewarding part of my career, as I knew what I produced would be used there and then to help protect life.

The most memorable character I worked alongside was a cheeky chappie by the name of Martin 'Jock' Harris who hailed from Kirkcaldy. As I got off the train at Cosford station to start my course, I was greeted by this ginger-headed Scot who stuck out his hand saying, 'Hi, I'm Martin Harris, Jock to you'. My first impression was 'I'm not going to get along with you, gobby!' But over the period of our course you couldn't help but love the guy. He was up to all sorts of tricks and made everyone laugh. He also got posted to JARIC at the end of our course and we worked together for years. I never saw him without a smile and everyone loved him. However, in March 1985 he was killed, whilst representing the RAF, taking part in a motorcycle sidecar race. He was only 25 years old but had packed so much into his short life and is still remembered by a trophy presented to the sportsman who has shown the best piece of sportsmanship over the previous 12 months. A great man and a great loss felt by the whole of Trade Group 14.

The most abiding memory of my time in the RAF is the true comradeship that is evident throughout our trade, which is still there today, several decades after I joined up. Unfortunately, the past few years have seen the passing of several of our most respected colleagues, and there is always a fantastic turnout at these sad funerals. The ease with which conversation carries on is a feeling which is not replicated anywhere else I can think of. To be able to do this after such a period of absence is remarkable to say the least. It only seems like yesterday when talking to my ex-RAF workmates. That's something I will treasure till my dying day.

RADAR

Radar is now a commonplace tool used in a variety of equipment. Its development played a crucial role in the history of the RAF and the UK.

Ground-based radar

The work of scientist Robert Watson-Watt and his team provided the Chain Home series of radars in time for the Luftwaffe offensive of 1940. They formed part of the world's first air defence detection, communication and control system, called the Dowding System after its commander, Air Chief Marshal Dowding. The radar installations, along with the Observer Corps stations, passed information on incoming enemy aircraft to Fighter Command's HQ at Bentley Priory, where this was filtered to determine genuine raids and then plotted on a map depicting the controlled area. Information was then quickly disseminated to the groups and sector operations rooms and then onto the airfields where fighters were launched.

When the Luftwaffe switched to night raids, the visual aspect of the system, the Observer Corps, was mainly rendered ineffective. Advancements in 360-degree scanning radar allowed overland radar coverage (the Chain Home of 1940 was only viable in detecting over the sea) and also gave a plan view of the aircraft's position. This led to ground-controlled interception units that directed night fighters to their targets through interception controllers.

After the war radar was also used for detecting incoming missiles. Fylingdales in the Yorkshire moorland was part of an early warning system designed to track Soviet ballistic missiles and then trigger for warning and retaliation. The site opened in 1963 and the 'golf balls' containing the radar scanners were a landmark of the area. They were replaced in the 1990s by the Solid State Phased Array, which can track 800 targets simultaneously at a distance of 3,000 miles.

Air-to-air radar

The first British air-to-air radars were fitted to night fighters, for Beaufighters attempting to intercept German bombers. Radar sets using microwave frequencies improved performance when introduced and gave the RAF a lead in air-to-air radar technology. Introduced in 1942, the Mark VIII set gave a range of about 5 miles.

Vampire and Meteor night fighters were equipped with radar, but the first British fighter to use avionics as an integral part of its weapons systems was the Javelin when it entered service in 1956. Its role was to intercept Soviet bombers; it used an AI.17 radar which gave indications of the target's location on the pilot's instruments.

The next step was the AI.23, part of the airborne interception radar and pilot's attack sight system (AIRPASS) of the English Electric Lightning, which entered service in 1960. Connecting the radar through a computer to the gunsight to give the pilot cueing information to then fire the aircraft's missiles, the AI.23 was also the world's first monopulse radar, which offered better performance (giving bearing and elevation data from one pulse) and could detect a Soviet bomber at a range of 40 miles.

The F-4 Phantom's introduction to the RAF brought with it pulse-Doppler radar systems, which gave better detection of low-flying targets. The aircraft also had beyond visual range (BVR) capability with its Sparrow missiles.

GREAT AIRCRAFT: MCDONNELL DOUGLAS F-4 PHANTOM

Maximum speed: 1,386 mph
Maximum altitude: 60,000 ft
Armament: 4 x Sparrow (or Skyflash), 4 x Sidewinder AAM; external 20 mm cannon, rocket pods, freefall bombs
Crew: 2

As in America the UK's Phantoms were operated by both navy and air force. The Phantom in RAF service came in the FG.1 variant, which was the type outlined for use by the Fleet Air Arm. The FGR.2 version began in the ground attack and reconnaissance roles but was later utilised solely in the fighter role. Fifteen squadrons operated the F-4, which formed the backbone of the UK's air defence from the mid-1970s until it was replaced by the Tornado F.3. The last F-4 left UK service in 1992.

The next air-to-air radar in the RAF's inventory was the AI.24 Foxhunter, designed for the interceptor version of the Tornado. There were problems and delays and the first production Tornado F.2s flew with concrete ballast instead of the radar, leading some to call the radar 'Blue Circle' after the cement manufacturer.

Typhoons currently use the Captor-M radar, which will be replaced by an AESA (active electronically scanned array) radar. The Captor-E radar is electronically scanned rather than the radar's antenna moving mechanically; it will give a field of view of 200 degrees. It can also provide simultaneous ground-to-air and air-to-air coverage. AESA radars are harder to jam and detect through radar warning receivers.

Tail warning radars

A key element of survivability in the air is being aware of potential attackers. Small tail warning radars such as Orange Putter were installed on Canberras, Vulcans and Valiants, although they were not regarded as wholly effective.

Radar warning receivers

One of the disadvantages of using radar is that it can be detected by the target aircraft. Radar warning receivers (RWR) are a key piece of equipment that would alert the crew when the aircraft had been detected by a hostile ground or air radar. In the Second World War Lancasters carried 'Boozer' RWR. An example of a more recent installation is that on the F-4 Phantom. The Marconi RWR was installed on top of the tailfin and gave them an appearance distinct from other F-4s.

Airborne early warning radar

The first use of airborne early warning (AEW) radar in the UK was the 1950s Fleet Air Arm Skyraiders fitted with the AN/APS-20. The same radar was fitted to the Fairey Gannet AEW.3 from 1960, which operated from the navy's carriers. When they were due to be withdrawn in the 1970s, the gap in coverage was filled by RAF Avro Shackletons, converted by having the same radar fitted. The Shackleton AEW.2 entered service in 1972. The radar was not effective in detecting low-level aircraft such as the Soviet Union's Sukhoi Su-24 Fencer over land. Pulse-Doppler radars were required.

WHEN THINGS DON'T GO RIGHT: NIMROD AEW

The USA had developed its airborne early warning and control system (AWACS) aircraft based on the Boeing 707 airframe and designated E-3. Its radar was capable of detecting targets 250 miles away and its pulse-Doppler capability provided the opportunity to detect low-level targets. NATO wished to buy the E-3, but Britain deliberated before in March 1977 it chose to develop its own AEW capability, based on the Nimrod airframe and using two radomes, one at either end of the fuselage. In 1980 the Nimrod AEW.3 flew for the first time, but there were problems with the integration of the systems that proved to be insurmountable, and the project was cancelled in 1986 at a cost estimated to be £1 billion.

The E-3D was ordered, the first of which arrived at Waddington in 1990.

GROUND-TO-AIR RADAR

Terrain-following radar (TFR)

In 1960, when the Soviet Union shot down the Lockheed U-2 flown by Francis Gary Powers, it forced a rethink. The use of surface-to-air missiles (SAMs) by the Soviets showed that the previous planned use of high-altitude bombing was no longer as viable, so V-bomber squadrons were instructed to practise low-level flying. To fly beneath the radar would allow an opportunity for attacking aircraft. One of the developments brought in and fitted to the Vulcan was TFR, which would give the crews the ability to fly at night at low level. The Tornado added another dimension to TFR, this being coupled to the autopilot to allow hands-free flying, enabling the aircraft to fulfil its day/night penetration role.

Synthetic aperture radar (SAR)

SAR uses digital technology to produce high-resolution images. It is used along with a ground moving target indicator (GMTI) in the Raytheon Sentinel R.1 as part of its airborne stand-off radar (ASTOR) system. It allows the Sentinel to provide ground commanders with up-to-date situational awareness.

WEAPONS

As a fighting force the air force has used a wide variety of weapons that employ increased levels of technological development, allowing great destructive capacity and accuracy.

Surface-to-air missile

Following the Second World War there was a move away from artillery in airfield defence to the primary defence weapon being the surface-to-air missile. Several were used by the RAF:

Tigercat

Developed from the navy's Seacat, the short-range Tigercat was in service from 1967 to 1978. It was manually guided by a ground-based operator.

Bloodhound

This entered service in 1958 as a second line of defence for V-bomber bases behind air defence fighters. Bloodhounds were powered by ramjets once they had been launched via booster rockets. The Mark I could reach speeds of Mach 2.2 while its successor, the Mark II, went to Mach 2.7. The Mark II was capable of shooting down aircraft from altitudes of 100 to 60,000 ft. It was the UK's main SAM throughout the Cold War but with the threat of Soviet attack receding, it was retired in 1991.

Rapier

Entering service in 1974 the Rapier is a short-range, low-level SAM, and replaced the Tigercat and the Bofors gun. To begin with, the missile was manually controlled from the ground by an operator using an optical guidance method. Radar guidance was brought in with the Blindfire version.

Precision-guided munitions

Many different methods were employed during the Second World War to improve accuracy, but it wasn't until the 1960s that a step change in weaponry was first seen in Vietnam with the laser-guided bomb (LGB). The Paveway used a laser designator to illuminate the target, and the 'smart' bomb would then be guided down the reflected laser's energy by a seeker head with canards acting as flight controls. The RAF first used LGBs (dropped by Harrier GR.3s) in the Falklands.

During the 1991 Gulf War, Buccaneers were sent to designate targets for Tornado GR.1s with Pave Spike until the aircraft's own thermal imaging airborne laser designator (TIALD) pods were introduced. During the latter stage of Operation Granby, 60 per cent of Tornado missions were using LGBs. Paveways are carried by both Tornado and Typhoon as well as the Reaper RPAS.

DID YOU KNOW?

During the Gulf War in 2003, inert bombs were dropped using precision-guided equipment, as the force of impact was enough to cause sufficient damage without the use of explosives, and there was less danger of collateral damage.

UNGUIDED MUNITIONS

For most of the RAF's history, munitions were dropped without any further guidance possible after release.

Bombs

In the First World War the bombs first used were small enough to be dropped by hand. By the end the largest bomb was the 1,650 lb weapon carried by the Handley Page O/400 bomber.

Most of the bombs dropped by the RAF in the Second World War were 500 and 1,000 lb bombs, with over 400,000 of the former and over a quarter of a million of the latter. Larger bombs were used in the form of 'cookies' of 4,000, 8,000 and 12,000 lb. These were supplemented by special weapons designed by Barnes Wallis.

Name	Weight (lb)	Details
Tallboy	12,000	The Tallboy was an 'earthquake' bomb that would penetrate the ground before exploding. It was successfully used against the *Tirpitz*, the V1 and V2 sites, and the Saumur railway tunnel.
Grand Slam	22,000	Developed from the Tallboy, less than 50 were used. The most powerful individual weapon before the atomic weapons in Japan. Used against the Bielefeld viaduct in March 1945.
Upkeep	9,250	Only used in one raid, on the Ruhr dams in 1943. Bomb was spun mechanically and then dropped at a precise height to allow it to bounce towards the target and then drop to a predetermined depth before exploding.

Cluster bombs

Phantoms, Harriers and Jaguars were equipped with the Hunting BL755 bomb, which consisted of a casing able to eject 147 bomblets. In the Falklands, Harrier GR.3s successfully dropped cluster bombs on Argentinian artillery positions at Goose Green. Due to the Convention on Cluster Munitions of 2010, the cluster bomb is no longer part of the RAF's inventory.

Unguided rockets

For ground attack the move to precision-guided munitions has led to the withdrawal of some types, such as the unguided rocket. Used with great effect by naval strike Mosquitoes and Beaufighters and ground attack Typhoons in the Second World War, they continued to be used by Harriers in Afghanistan, with the CRV-7 rocket capable of Mach 3 speeds.

JP233

The Hunting JP233 was an airfield denial weapon, contained in a large pod carried by Tornadoes. The Tornado flew low over the target before releasing the small munitions from the weapon. The weapon came in two forms: anti-runway sub-munitions weighing 57 lb each, of which 30 were carried in the rear of the weapon. They were to crater the runway surface. In the front section, 215 anti-personnel mines were carried, each weighing 5½ lb. The JP233 was heavily used in 1991 during the initial stage of the Gulf War but was withdrawn following the United Kingdom's signing of the Mine Ban Treaty in 1997.

Nuclear

> *'I believe the only really sound course would be to build up a completely overwhelming British/ American bomber force with the A-bomb capable of pulverising Russia itself and eliminating the Red Air Force at its bases.'*
> **MARSHAL OF THE RAF SIR JOHN SLESSOR, 1952**

Immediately after the Second World War the United Kingdom government made the decision that it should develop its own nuclear weapons, in order to secure its position internationally as a major nation.

When the USA legislated that it would not share its nuclear secrets, British scientists who had assisted with building the bombs used on

Hiroshima and Nagasaki were able to contribute to Britain's nuclear weapons programme. The first bomb was exploded in 1952 off the coast of Australia and the first live air drop was successfully carried out in 1956.

The first nuclear weapons – the atomic bombs – while enormously powerful were superseded by the hydrogen (or thermonuclear) bombs. These reached much higher 'yields'. The bomb used at Hiroshima had a yield of 12.5 kilotons (equivalent weight of TNT) but Britain's hydrogen bombs reached the megaton range, i.e., 1 million tons. The UK's first hydrogen bomb was dropped on 8 November 1957 at Christmas Island in the Pacific..

The means of delivery were to be provided by a series of specifically designed jet 'V-bombers': Valiant, Victor and Vulcan. Valiants were first in service in 1955, but were withdrawn 10 years later after cracks were detected in their wing spars. The Victors were later converted to the aerial tanker role and the Vulcan remained the only V-bomber in the nuclear role. When the navy submarine force took over the strategic nuclear deterrence role in 1969, the RAF continued with tactical nuclear weapons. Vulcans, Tornadoes, Jaguars and Buccaneers carried the WE.177 freefall bomb.

Nuclear weapons carried by RAF aircraft:

Name	Date introduced	Details	Nuclear warhead
Blue Danube	1953	RAF's first atomic weapon. Freefall. Withdrawn in 1962.	10–40 kilotons
Red Beard	1958	Tactical weapon, issued to Canberra squadrons as well as V-bomber units. The Fleet Air Arm also had Red Beards. Replaced by WE.177.	15 kilotons (Mark 1) 25 kilotons (Mark 2)

Violet Club	1958	A short-term 'interim' weapon in the megaton range introduced before Yellow Sun was ready. Only 12 were delivered. Similar in appearance to Blue Danube.	500 kilotons
Yellow Sun	1958	Freefall. Designed to be the UK's first megaton weapon. Main nuclear bomb carried by V-bombers before Blue Steel. Withdrawn in 1969.	0.5 megatons (Mark 1) 1 megaton (Mark 2)
Project E: Mark 7, 28, 43	1958	The USA offered nuclear weapons as a stopgap. They were jointly administered by the UK and the USA. A number of Project E bombs were deployed before being phased out in 1960.	(Information not released)
Blue Steel	1963	Stand-off missile. After being dropped at 35,000 ft the missile was propelled by its own rockets to Mach 2.3 before climbing to 70,000 ft. It then dived to its target. The range was 150 miles. Techniques were later used to launch from low level, where its range was reduced to 50 miles. Withdrawn in 1970.	1 megaton

WE.177	1966	Strategic or tactical use. For low-level use by loft bombing or retarded by parachute. Operated by Vulcan, Buccaneer and Jaguar. The WE.177A version was used by the navy. Withdrawn in 1998, ending the RAF's nuclear capability.	A: 0.5–10 kilotons B: 450 kilotons (V-force only). Replaced Yellow Sun Mk 2 in strategic role. C: 200 kilotons

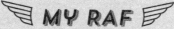

MY RAF

TONY CUNNANE
Squadron Leader, served 1953–2001

I joined the air force because with national service rapidly approaching, the RAF wrote the best and most appealing answer to my written request for more information and gave me an all-expenses-paid trip to London to attend the Aircrew Selection Centre then at RAF Hornchurch. I enjoyed almost every minute of my initial training: both the square bashing at RAF Bridgnorth and the superb technical training at RAF Locking.

Without a shadow of a doubt, the greatest privilege I had was in 1993 when I was organising at Scampton the 50th Anniversary of the Dams Raid and enjoyed the company of all the then surviving men who had flown on the raid. I had been in awe of them all from the very day the Dams Raid was reported in the newspapers and on the BBC the day after the raid (I was seven years old then).

I am still astonished that a poor, very shy, working-class boy like me, initially with a broad Yorkshire accent, whose main ambition at school was to become a professional musician – thwarted by family matters outside my control – was able to progress through an amazing series of appointments in the RAF. I went from Ground Wireless Fitter to Air Signaller (Shackletons) to Air Electronics Officer (Valiants) to Pilot (Jet Provosts, Hunters and Victors).

For me the best aspect of being in the air force was when the recruiting literature in 1953 stated, 'Join the RAF and see the world'. Well I did. Sadly, you can't do that these days!

Nuclear missiles

The German V2 had demonstrated the destructive power of long-range missiles and the difficulties in interception. When the decision was made for Britain to have its own nuclear deterrent, the technology to build its own ballistic missiles was not available, but attempts were made for the RAF to be equipped with its own missiles:

▶ Thor: Thor was an American-produced intermediate range ballistic missile (IRBM). It was 'dual control', i.e. jointly controlled by the UK and USA. The missile had a 1,500-mile range and 60 were deployed in RAF service. Although it was deemed effective, it was vulnerable to enemy attack, being stationed permanently above ground, and it also took 15 minutes to prepare for firing. It was withdrawn in 1963.

▶ Blue Streak: The operational requirement was issued in 1955 and Blue Streak was to avoid the vulnerability suffered by Thor in being stationed in silos underground. Expected to be in service by 1964, the project ended in 1960 as its fixed sites were felt to be still too vulnerable.

▶ Skybolt: The American Skybolts were proposed as a cheaper form of deterrence than Blue Streak. They were ballistic missiles, air-launched by V-bombers, and were projected to have a 1,000-mile range. The project was cancelled in 1962 when the USA decided to pursue intercontinental ballistic missiles (ICBMs) as its chief deterrent. The USA offered Britain the opportunity to continue developing Skybolt, but this was rejected and the UK decided to purchase US ICBMs in the form of the submarine-launched Polaris.

DID YOU KNOW?

Work on Skybolt was not completely wasted as when Shrike anti-radar missiles were fitted to Vulcans in the Falklands conflict, they were able to use wiring provided for the Skybolt.

Guns

The First World War began with aircrew taking their own side arms and rifles into the air for aerial combat as their aeroplanes carried no defensive armament. Machine guns presented their own challenges: when fired on the 'pusher' type of aeroplane the ejected cartridge shells were blown by the airstream into the propeller. There was also the issue of the gunner having to move around in an open cockpit with the very real risk of falling out during evasive manoeuvres.

For 'tractor' aeroplanes a means had to be found of firing them through the propeller arc. At first metal plates were fitted to the propeller blades until synchronisation ensured the bullets passed through the space between the spinning blades. Fighter pilots also faced the problems of having to change ammunition drums for Lewis guns in flight or attempting to fix jammed belts for the Vickers guns. The calibre of these weapons was the same as the Lee Enfield rifle: 0.303 of an inch and this continued through the interwar period and into the Second World War with the Spitfires and Hurricanes.

During the Battle of Britain the effectiveness of German cannons was not missed by those on the receiving end. Cannons were tried on Spitfires but were not a success until teething problems were sorted out for later marks. The 20 mm-calibre cannon was the standard weapon for later piston-engined fighters and into the jet age with the Meteor. The 20 mm Hispano cannon was superseded by the 30 mm Aden cannon with double the rate of fire.

With the advent of air-to-air missiles, the gun was no longer regarded as necessary. Where initial designs had not provided for aircraft to carry cannon, external pods were provided for aircraft such as the Harrier, Phantom and Hawk. The Phantom used an SUU-23 pod containing the Gatling gun-type Vulcan 20 mm cannon.

DID YOU KNOW?

An anti-tank gun was fitted in the Mosquito. Nicknamed 'Tsetse', the Mosquito XVIII had a 57 mm Molins gun fitted in the nose in place of its four 20 mm cannon for anti-shipping strikes.

DID YOU KNOW?

One of the explanations sometimes offered for the expression 'given the full nine yards' comes from the distance between the Avro Lancaster's ammunition box and the rear gunner's position.

Missiles

The advent of electronic guidance equipment and rocket power plants small enough to be carried by a jet resulted in a plethora of new weapons.

Air-to-surface missiles:

▶ Anti-radiation missiles: Anti-radiation missiles are designed to be fired at radar stations through detecting transmitted radio waves. The aircraft carrying them operate in the suppression of enemy air defences (SEAD) role. They were introduced into combat during the Vietnam War with the American AGM-45A Shrike. The AGM-88A HARM, introduced in 1983, was capable of Mach 2 speeds. The British developed their own weapon with the BAE-Marconi air-launched anti-radiation missile (ALARM) carried by Tornadoes. Its mode of operation was to zoom-climb to 40,000 ft and then deploy its parachute before locking on to its target. It would then release its parachute before diving on to the target. If the enemy radar was switched off, internal guidance would continue to direct the missile. First used in the Gulf War of 1991, it was retired from RAF service in 2013.

▶ Anti-shipping missiles: As seen in the Falklands conflict in 1982, anti-shipping missiles can be effective weapons that are difficult to counter. The Argentinian navy used the French-built Exocet missile, which was similar to the Martel, carried by Buccaneers. The Martel used TV-guidance or passive radiation seeking. It was replaced by Sea Eagle, which had a longer range and was a 'fire and forget' weapon with its own radar that meant the attacking aircraft could launch further away from enemy defence systems. It was withdrawn from service in 1999.

Air-to-air missiles

Getting bullets to hit an evasive aerial target was historically one of the most challenging tasks that faced the combat pilot. One solution was for the attacking aircraft to launch rocket-powered missiles that would prove difficult to evade.

▸ Infrared (IR): The first British IR air-to-air missile (AAM) was the Firestreak, introduced in 1958 as part of the Gloster Javelin's armament. Its seeker detected heat from the target's engines. The Lightning was also equipped with both Firestreak and the Red Top missile. (Both missiles were given irreverent nicknames by pilots: Firewood and Red Flop.) The step change in IR missiles came with the American-produced AIM-9 Sidewinder, used by the Fleet Air Arm's Scimitar and then the F-4 Phantom. Navy Sea Harriers were fitted with Sidewinders and on the eve of the Falklands conflict were given a more up-to-date AIM-9L version, offering all-aspect detection of a target, which meant an enemy could be attacked from a head-on position rather than the traditional approach from behind. The new generation of short-range AAM came in the form of the AIM-132 advanced short-range air-to-air missile (ASRAAM). This could be launched before lock-on was achieved, relying on its own IR sensor for guidance to the target.

▸ Radar-guided: The USA's AIM-4 Falcon of the early 1960s was the world's first radar-guided missile. It was superseded by the

BVR AIM-7 Sparrow, which had a range of 12 miles. It was a 'beam-riding' missile in that the parent aircraft 'painted' the target with its own radar and the missile's aerials collected guidance information from the launch aircraft and directed it towards the target. However, it was not a 'fire and forget' missile, and if radar lock was lost the missile would miss. Sparrows equipped the Phantom until they were replaced by the Skyflash in 1978. The next generation in missile technology was the AIM-120 advanced medium range air-to-air missile (AMRAAM). Developed in the 1980s, it carried its own radar and used IFF (Identification Friend or Foe) to detect and identify its target, aided by the launch aircraft's radar. It has a range of over 20 miles. AMRAAMs were first used by the USAF in the Gulf War of 1991 and were procured for use by the Sea Harrier and Tornado F.3. Typhoons currently carry AIM-120s.

NAVIGATIONAL AIDS

Early aircraft carried compasses, but these were not wholly reliable. Railway lines were useful guides to follow and if necessary pilots could fly low enough to read the station names. Matters improved with the map, compass and stopwatch becoming a tried-and-tested method of navigation taught in elementary flying training. Astronavigation with sextants was used but was not always effective in wartime conditions. Identification of ground features to ascertain accuracy of position was key to this method, but when night bombing it could prove to be problematic. In the Second World War one of the major problems Bomber Command faced was the lack of accuracy when it switched to night-time attacks. So technological means were introduced to improve navigation to the target and then delivery of weapons.

GEE

A raid on Essen saw the first operational use of GEE. Two UK ground transmitters sent pulsed signals that were received on board the bomber. These signals, when plotted on a chart, could provide a fix of the aircraft's position. Accuracy varied on range from the transmitters, but a few hundred yards was possible at its maximum of 350 miles. It was also useful for aircraft finding their way home and was used throughout the war. A development called GEE-H was used after the war by Canberras.

Oboe

Oboe provided a blind-bombing facility. Two radio beams were transmitted from UK ground stations. The bomber flew along an arc provided by one of the beams, and its position was tracked by operators. When it crossed the second beam, the operator sent signals that released the bomber's weapons. Oboe was accurate but could only be used by one bomber at a time and so was normally utilised by a Pathfinder Mosquito that would mark the target for the approaching bomber stream. Its maximum range was 300 miles.

H2S

Introduced in January 1943 each bomber could carry its own H2S radar set in a housing under the fuselage. H2S provided a picture of the ground ahead and in poor weather would give accurate results. As with any radar H2S could be detected and German night fighters were given airborne radar detection equipment. As it did not rely on receiving a signal from the UK it did not suffer range restrictions.

NBS

The H2S was retained into the 1950s (and beyond) as part of the Avro Vulcan's navigation and bombing system (NBS). Its location information was combined with data from another radar measuring drift and ground speed, to calculate the bomb release point. Steering indications were sent to the pilot to follow and the bombs were then released automatically.

INS

In the 1960s technology advanced with the advent of inertial navigation systems (INS). Accelerometers and gyroscopes were used to determine position without use of external reference gathering via radar. The Harrier GR.1 was the first RAF aircraft to be equipped with INS (later the Jaguar and Phantom FGR.2 were similarly equipped). It could be prone to errors unless updated with accurate position fixing. In the Harrier, the INS was used to update a moving map display, another first for RAF pilots.

GPS

Accurate position information is now mostly provided through global positioning system (GPS), which uses transmissions from multiple satellites. The Harrier GR.9's avionics were upgraded with an INS coupled to GPS to ensure greater accuracy. The Storm Shadow missile has GPS incorporated into its avionics.

TACAN

Derived from wartime Oboe, tactical air navigation (TACAN) is an ultra high frequency (UHF) system that uses ground-based beacons to transmit range and bearing information to the receiving aircraft. Guidance information is received in the cockpit which aids en route navigation and landing approaches. Air-to-air TACAN is also used, particularly in aerial refuelling tankers.

DID YOU KNOW?

During the Second World War a simple but effective innovation aided aircraft returning in fog. Fog investigation and dispersal operation (FIDO) consisted of two lines, containing petrol, which ran along the length of the runway; when set alight they allowed pilots a clear sight of where to land.

TARGETING EQUIPMENT
In the First World War weapons were initially aimed by Mark One Eyeball, then dropped over the side of the aircraft's fuselage when the pilot or observer judged it the right moment. Bombsights were introduced such as the course-setting bomb sight, which took into account the effects of wind. It was widely used even into the Second World War. Creating a gyro-stabilised bombsight able to be operated easily by a bomb aimer took time, and it wasn't until 1942 that the Mark XIV became Bomber Command's standard bombsight; it was used in aircraft like the Lancaster and remained in RAF service up until 1965.

Despite all this technological advancement, one famous wartime method of targeting that could easily be described as low-tech was also stunningly effective. In the attack on the Ruhr dams of 16/17 May 1943, one of 617 Sqn's bomb aimers used a simple bombsight: a v-shaped piece of wood which they held up to their eye. At each end of the piece of wood was a narrow piece of metal, the position of which was designed to line up with towers on the dam. When it did so the aircraft was at the correct bombing distance and the 'bouncing bomb' was released. The device was used by Pilot Officer John Fort in AJ-J and it was this Lancaster's bomb that finally breached the Möhne Dam.

FLIR and NVG
The ability to see the target at night has been a challenge since the early days of night bombing. Parachute flares were used during the Second World War and in peacetime during the 1960s and 1970s Canberras and Harriers practised dropping Lepus flares that gave 2.8 million candlepower of light. Flares could be effective but the attackers suffered the disadvantage of announcing their attack and the accompanying risk of a possible loss of night vision.

Thermal-imaging technology brought in a new era for night flying. The C-130 Hercules transport and Chinook helicopter crews were the first to use night vision goggles (NVG) that amplified available light. The Harrier GR.7 version was designed to have an enhanced night capability, and its pilots were equipped with NVG. While they were certainly a useful tool, they did present an obstacle to crew safety in that during an ejection their weight, when magnified by the rapid acceleration forces, could cause severe injury to the wearer. A solution was found in that when ejection was initiated the goggles themselves would be ejected from the pilot's helmet.

The GR.7 also came with forward-looking infrared (FLIR), giving a picture on a screen in the cockpit from a sensor mounted on the nose. Many current fighters use infrared search and track (IRST) systems that detect targets without the use of radar. As IR is a passive system it does not emit radiation, unlike radar, and so can be used when a pilot does not wish to give away their aircraft's position.

The Typhoon has passive infrared airborne tracking equipment (PIRATE) mounted on the front of the aircraft's fuselage, which offers detection of air-to-air and air-to-ground targets.

ELECTRONIC COUNTERMEASURES (ECM)

The Second World War was the first conflict with electronics used as a weapon. Lancasters carried 'Airborne Cigar' equipment which jammed German radio broadcasts with a warbling sound, while the Germans' Freya air defence radar was jammed by Mandrel equipment.

In the post-war period the Soviet Union's fighter control technology was not thought to be complicated and countermeasures came in the form of Green Palm, an electronic jammer that worked across the limited number of frequencies the Soviet Union used. The 1960s required a greater level of technology as defences increased in complexity, so the Vulcan was fitted with Red Shrimp ECM between the aircraft's starboard engine jet pipes. Before taking part in the Black Buck missions, Vulcans were fitted with the AN/ALQ-101D ECM pod as the Red Shrimp would have not been capable of dealing with all the threats Argentinian ground defences would pose.

As for current aircraft, the Tornado carries a dedicated Sky Shadow ECM pod on one of its wing pylons. Sky Shadow is autonomous and responds automatically to perceived threats. The pod has been upgraded since its inception and carries two towed radar decoys (TRDs). The Typhoon is also equipped with TRDs, which form part of its defensive aids sub-system alongside flares, chaff and electronic jamming.

DID YOU KNOW?

In 1961 during a large-scale exercise called Sky Shield II, a force of Vulcans made mock attacks on America and one was able to reach New York undetected, as the aircraft in the formation used electronic jamming to shield its track.

SAFETY AND PROTECTION

Technological advances have not just served the needs of operational aspects of the RAF; they have also increased the safety of aircrew.

Ejection seats

The advent of jet aircraft meant that higher speeds were attainable, and any aircrew escaping by simply opening the canopy and 'jumping over the side' would be very likely to hit the fin or another part of the aircraft. Rocket-powered ejection seats were developed which could rapidly pull a pilot or navigator away from a stricken aircraft. At first they had speed and altitude limits but later seats are described as 'zero-zero', i.e. they could operate effectively at zero altitude and zero speed.

DID YOU KNOW?

Any aircrew who eject using a Martin-Baker seat are given a tie by the seat manufacturer and admitted to the Ejection Tie Club.

RAF TRADITIONS

Binbrook Boots

At Binbrook the flying boots of pilots who had successfully ejected were screwed to the ceiling of the officer's mess. The tradition started when a French Mirage pilot on approach to the airfield ejected after suffering an engine failure and in doing so lost one of his boots. When the station was closed the boots were moved to a nearby pub. When the pub changed ownership the boots were removed and 'The French Lieutenant's Boot' was returned to its former wearer.

DID YOU KNOW?

Nuclear bomber crews were issued with eye patches. This was to prevent them being completely blinded if they inadvertently looked at the flash of a nuclear explosion.

FLYING CLOTHING

In 1918 every aircraft had an open cockpit. Flying gear consisted of leather jackets and trousers, with helmets and gloves.

Matters improved with the Sidcot suit (named after its designer, future photographic reconnaissance advocate Sidney Cotton). It was an overall with a fur lining and was used into the Second World War. Part of the aircrew's apparel was the silk scarf, which has become part of the iconography of the RAF. While it offered a dash of colour, it was worn for practical purposes: to prevent the neck chafing that came through constantly turning to spot other aircraft. Scarves also stopped cold air entering the suit.

During the Battle of Britain, which took place in summer, pilots would fly in their uniforms, with a life-saving waistcoat – the famous yellow 'Mae West' – and their flying helmets. While comfortable, this did not offer much protection against the real possibility of in-flight fires. Hurricane and Spitfire fuel tanks were situated in front of the pilot and horrific burns could ensue if these were hit. Pilots who ditched also learned not to wear a collar and tie as the seawater tended to make them contract in size.

DID YOU KNOW?

Aircrew flying in open cockpits in hot and sunny regions in the 1920s and 1930s wore an adapted pith helmet to prevent sunburn.

As aircraft flew higher it added to the challenges facing aircrew. Sheepskin jackets and trousers offered some protection against the colder temperatures, but for rear gunners who were sitting still for long periods the cold was always an issue. Electrical heating of boots, gloves and waistcoats worn inside the suit was welcomed – when it worked – but the main challenge at altitude was hypoxia, so oxygen-breathing systems were introduced. The early oxygen apparatus employed a constant-flow system, which used up twice as much oxygen as the German regulator equipment. In 1940 successful tests were carried out on the Economiser, also known as 'the Puffing Billy', which regulated the flow of oxygen.

Flying in unpressurised aircraft at height could result in 'the bends' (decompression sickness occurs when bubbles form in the bloodstream or tissues), so pressurised cockpits were introduced. Lightning pilots, expected to make high-altitude interceptions, were given specialised equipment to allow them to survive a cockpit depressurisation.

G-suits

Equipment to alleviate the effects of acceleration on the human body was developed during the Second World War as pilots were losing consciousness in high-G manoeuvres. Research by the RAF Physiological Laboratory showed blood was pooling away from the brain, so these predecessors of the modern-day G-suit used water bladders to prevent blood pooling, thus increasing the amount of G that could be sustained.

Immersion suit

The immersion suit was introduced to help aircrew forced to eject over water. Made of rubber it preserved body temperatures and increased the amount of time the wearer could survive in the water. The immersion suit was worn over the normal flying suit and was secured by tight rubber seals at neck, cuff and ankle to prevent water ingress. A thermal garment nicknamed the 'bunny suit' could be worn underneath.

NBC (nuclear, biological, chemical)

In the case of nuclear, biological or chemical attack, aircrew were issued with charcoal-lined clothing designed to protect them against such threats. They wore an inner NBC coverall and the Aircrew Respirator No. 5, a mask designed to operate with a flying helmet.

HELMETS

With the increase in speed and use of ejection seats in the post-war period, in order to protect the head, 'bone domes', i.e. fibre-glass, one-piece helmets, were produced. Pilots had helmet-fitted visors, either clear or tinted. New helmet designs continued to be developed through the succeeding years, with the recent Typhoon Striker helmet having a helmet-mounted display (HMD) that allows the pilot to see flight and targeting information without having to look at the head-up display (HUD) or down into the cockpit. The radar, sensors such as infrared, and weapons can all be slaved to the helmet so that the pilot 'points' them wherever they look. They can then issue voice commands to lock on to targets.

The F-35 helmet is more advanced and offers the pilot a mix of flight data as seen in a normal HUD along with targeting information and sensor imagery, allowing freedom of head movement while having access to all the necessary information at all times. Part of the imagery presented comes from six infrared cameras mounted on the aircraft, allowing the pilot to look 'through' the fuselage to the ground or sea below.

PART 5

MEMORIALS

CHAPTER SIXTEEN

MEMORIALS

Memorials to those who have served and have suffered injury or been killed can be found the length and breadth of the country. The Imperial War Museums website lists over 840 memorials in the UK that commemorate those from the RAF. They can range in size and scope from a simple plaque to a particular individual, to a whole building, as at Runnymede.

The major memorials include:

RAF MEMORIAL

Unveiled: 1923

Location: Victoria Embankment, London

The official memorial of the RAF and its constituent services. It was established to mark the sacrifice of those in the First World War but is also used to commemorate those who died in the Second World War. The stone pylon is topped with a gilded eagle on top of a globe. Each year on Battle of Britain Sunday the Chief of Air Staff lays a wreath at the memorial, and on Remembrance Day a wreath in the shape of a pilot's brevet is attached to the memorial.

AIR FORCES MEMORIAL
Unveiled: 1953
Location: Runnymede, Surrey
More than 20,000 people gathered to witness the opening of this memorial, commemorating the 20,455 airmen and airwomen who died in the Second World War while based in the UK or Europe and who also have no known grave. The memorial is in the form of a cloister with each individual's name engraved in stone.

BOMBER COMMAND MEMORIAL
Unveiled: 2012
Location: Green Park, London
The official memorial to the 55,573 men who died in Bomber Command during the Second World War. It consists of the bronze sculptures of a crew of seven aircrew. The roof over the statues includes aluminium parts of the wreckage of a Handley Page Halifax bomber that was shot down over Belgium in 1944.

THE BATTLE OF BRITAIN MONUMENT
Unveiled: 2005
Location: Victoria Embankment, London
This frieze depicts various figures from the battle in bronze: pilots, mechanics, gunners, WAAFs, female factory workers, Observer Corps, civilians sheltering from the Blitz and rescue workers. It is over 80 ft long. The monument was funded by public subscription and a contribution from the government of the Czech Republic.

NATIONAL MEMORIAL TO THE FEW
Unveiled: 1993
Location: Capel-le-Ferne, Kent
Battle of Britain pilot Geoffrey Page was the inspiration for the memorial which is situated at 'Hellfire Corner', the area that saw much

of the fighting during the initial stages of the battle. The memorial features a statue depicting a pilot looking out over the English Channel, a bust of Keith Park, a wall with the names of those aircrew who flew in the battle, a visitor centre and a replica Spitfire and Hurricane.

POLISH WAR MEMORIAL
Unveiled: 1948
Location: Northolt, London
It commemorates the 2,165 Polish aircrew who died in the Second World War flying as part of the Polish Air Force alongside the Allies.

RAF CHAPEL WITH MEMORIAL WINDOW
Unveiled: 1947
Location: Westminster Abbey, London
Dedicated to those who lost their lives while in the service during the Battle of Britain. The committee set up to raise funds for the chapel and window in 1943 was headed by Lord Trenchard and Lord Dowding. The badges of each squadron that took part are represented in the stained glass windows.

RAF, COMMONWEALTH & ALLIED AIR FORCES MEMORIAL
Unveiled: 1989
Location: Plymouth Hoe
The memorial is a tribute to RAF, Commonwealth and Allied air force personnel who served in the Second World War. A bronze figure of an individual aircrew member stands on top of a Cornish granite plinth.

SAINT GEORGE'S ROYAL AIR FORCE CHAPEL OF REMEMBRANCE
Unveiled: 1951

Location: Biggin Hill

This famous fighter station is now home to the chapel constructed as a memorial to those who died in the Battle of Britain and other conflicts. A previous chapel had been constructed from prefab units in 1943 but was lost in a fire. The current chapel was dedicated in November 1951, and the memorial includes a Spitfire and a Hurricane.

OTHERS

Other memorials include:

Propeller blade and part of engine	RAF Hunsdon, Hertfordshire
Garden of Remembrance	National Memorial Arboretum, Staffordshire
Stone of Remembrance (RAF Regiment)	National Memorial Arboretum, Staffordshire
Book of Remembrance	Chedburgh, Suffolk
Hornbeam tree	Bury St Edmunds, Suffolk
Memorial window	St John the Baptist Church, North Luffenham, Rutland, Leicestershire
Plaque	RAF Swinderby, Lincolnshire
Replica Spitfire	Fairhaven Lake, Lytham St Annes, Lancashire
Spire and walls of remembrance	International Bomber Command Centre, Lincoln, Lincolnshire

INDIVIDUAL MEMORIALS
Lord Trenchard
Unveiled: 1961
Location: Victoria Embankment Gardens, London
This bronze statue of Trenchard in full dress uniform is located in front of the former Air Ministry building in Westminster.

Air Chief Marshal Sir Keith Park
Unveiled: 2010
Location: Waterloo Place, London
It took many years but eventually a statue was erected in tribute to the commander of 11 Group during the Battle of Britain. The New Zealander, known for visiting his squadrons in his own Hurricane, inspired the comment by Marshal of the RAF Lord Tedder, 'If ever any one man won the Battle of Britain, he did.' The bronze figure shows Park in flying gear and was unveiled on Battle of Britain Day.

Air Chief Marshal Hugh Dowding
Unveiled: 1988
Location: The Strand, London
This statue of Dowding was placed outside St Clement Danes Church in London. The church was damaged during the Blitz and restored through money donated by air force members. It is now the Central Church of the RAF and in that regard another important figure is marked with a statue outside: Marshal of the RAF Sir Arthur Harris.

Pilot Officer Lawrence Whitbread
Each year on 20 September, St Laurence's Church in Ludlow is floodlit in memory of Pilot Officer Lawrence Whitbread, who died on that day in 1940.

Squadron Leader Mike Stephens
On 27 September 1983 Tornado ZA586 of 9 Sqn flown by Squadron Leader Mike Stephens and Flight Lieutenant Nigel Nickles was returning from a night sortie when it suffered a total electrical

failure. Stephens ordered his navigator to eject, which he did, but was himself unable to escape the aircraft before it crashed near Wolferton in Norfolk. An oak tree was planted in his memory along with a commemorative plaque.

DID YOU KNOW?

Three roads at Biggin Hill were named in honour of the three WAAFs awarded the Military Medal in 1940: Mortimer Drive, Turner Avenue and Henderson Grove. Other streets in the area commemorate aircrew who died in the war.

THE FUTURE

In its 100 years the RAF has gone through severe challenges, politically, financially and militarily. Its personnel have faced enemy forces in numerous areas of the world, in the air and on the ground, but it is perhaps the one closest to home that has cemented its name in British folklore, when in 1940 it was seen as the last defence against Hitler's invasion plans in the Battle of Britain.

The RAF is a highly technical force, albeit one small in numbers. On 1 April 2015 the RAF had 31,830 full-time members (plus 2,220 Reserves) – a total less than in the middle of its post-First World War period in 1929 when it had just 34,250 personnel. At the end of the Cold War in 1989 there were 93,100 in uniform. While staffing levels are lower than in the past, the level of complexity in technology continues to rise, with unmanned aerial vehicles being just one example that has altered the way the air force goes into combat.

The basis on which the RAF is organised has also changed. In 2008 UK military flying training was outsourced to a public–private partnership. Ascent Flight Training (a joint venture between Lockheed Martin and Babcock International) was awarded a 25-year contract to provide the aircraft and infrastructure for all areas of military flying training: elementary, basic, fast-jet, multi-engine and rotary.

Other changes have seen the amalgamation of previously separate functions. 28 Sqn oversaw operational conversion of two types –

Puma and Chinook – and in 1999 the Joint Helicopter Command was formed with helicopters from the air force, navy and army. Before their withdrawal from service in 2010 Harriers were flown by navy and air force pilots as part of Joint Force Harrier. This arrangement will continue with the F-35B, with the commander of 617 Sqn being drawn alternately from the navy and air force.

Whatever shape the RAF takes on in the future, its personnel will undoubtedly continue to maintain the high standards of skill, determination and professionalism set by those who have worn the light blue uniform through its first century.

In April 1934 Marshal of the Royal Air Force Lord Trenchard performed the opening ceremony of Middlesex Auxiliary Air Force's town headquarters. In his speech Trenchard said one of the reasons he'd accepted the invitation was that he liked to think he wasn't forgotten. It is highly unlikely that Trenchard, and the organisation he had such an important part in establishing, will ever be in any danger of being forgotten.

SOURCES

BOOKS

Armitage, Michael, *The Royal Air Force: An Illustrated History* (Arms and Armour Press, 1996)

Bamford, Joe, *Tales from the Control Tower* (Fonthill Media, 2012)

Bishop, Patrick, *Bomber Boys: Fighting Back 1940–1945* (Harper Perennial, 2010)

Bishop, Patrick, *Wings: The RAF at War, 1912–2012* (Atlantic Books, 2013)

Bowyer, Chaz, *Coastal Command at War* (Ian Allan, 1979)

Bowyer, Chaz, *For Valour: The Air VCs* (Grub Street, 1992)

Congdon, Philip, *Per Ardua ad Astra: A Handbook of the Royal Air Force, 2nd edition* (Airlife, 1994)

Connelly, Mark, *Reaching for the Stars: A New History of Bomber Command in World War II* (I. B. Tauris, 2001)

Downing, Taylor, *Spies in the Sky: The Secret Battle for Aerial Intelligence during World War II* (Abacus, 2012)

Ethell, Jeffrey; Price, Alfred, *Air War South Atlantic* (Sidgwick and Jackson, 1983)

Finnegan, Terrence J., *Shooting the Front: Allied Aerial Reconnaissance in the First World War* (Spellmount, 2014)

Goodall, Philip, *My Target Was Leningrad V Force: Preserving Our Democracy'* (Fonthill Media, 2014)

Hall, Ian, *Tornado Boys: Thrilling Tales from the Men and Women Who Have Operated this Indomitable Modern-Day Bomber* (Grub Street, 2016)

Halley, James J., *The Squadrons of the Royal Air Force* (Air Britain Historians Ltd, 1980)

Hammerton, Sir John (ed.) *ABC of the RAF: Handbook for All Branches of the Air Force* (The Amalgamated Press Ltd, 1943)

Hering, Squadron Leader P. G., *Customs and Traditions of the Royal Air Force* (Gale and Polden Ltd, 1961)

James, A. G. Trevenen, *The Royal Air Force: The Past 30 Years* (Macdonald and Jane's, 1976)

Jarrett, Philip (ed.) *The Modern War Machine: Military Aviation since 1945* (Putnam Aeronautical Books, 2000)

Jefford, Wing Commander C. G., *RAF Squadrons: A Comprehensive Record of the Movement and Equipment of All RAF Squadrons and Their Antecedents since 1912* (Airlife, 1988)

Kendrick, Ian, *More Music in the Air* (MOD, 2010)

Marston, Bob, *Harrier Boys, Volume 1: Cold War through the Falklands 1969–1990* (Grub Street, 2015)

Marston, Bob, *Harrier Boys, Volume 2: New Technology, New Threats, New Tactics, 1990–2010* (Grub Street, 2016)

Overy, Richard, *Bomber Command 1939–1945: Reaping the Whirlwind* (Harper-Collins, 2000)

Pike, Richard, *The Lightning Boys: True Tales from Pilots of the English Electric Lightning* (Grub Street, 2011)

Rexford-Welch, (ed.) Squadron Leader S. C., *The Royal Air Force Medical Services Vol. 1, Administration* (HMSO, 1954)

Richards, Denis; Saunders, Hilary St George, *Royal Air Force, 1939–1945, Volume 1: The Fight at Odds* (HMSO, 1974)

Rood, Dr Graham, *A Brief History of Flying Clothing* (Journal of Aeronautical History, Paper No. 2014/01)

Ross, Wing Commander A. E., *Through Eyes of Blue: Personal Memories of the RAF from 1918* (Airlife, 2002)

Smith, Malcolm, *British Air Strategy Between the Wars* (Clarendon Press, 1984)

Smithies, Edward, *Aces, Erks and Backroom Boys: Personal Stories of Britain's Air War, 1939–45* (Cassell Military, 2002)

Taylor, John W. R.; Moyes, P. J. R., *Pictorial History of the RAF, Volume 1: 1918–1939* (Ian Allan, 1968)

Taylor, John W. R.; Moyes, P. J. R., *Pictorial History of the RAF, Volume 2: 1939–1945* (Ian Allan, 1969)

Taylor, John W. R.; Moyes, P. J. R., *Pictorial History of the RAF, Volume 3: 1945–1969* (Ian Allan, 1970)

Thetford, Owen, *Aircraft of the Royal Air Force since 1918* (Putnam and Company, 1979)

Wynn, Humphrey, *RAF Nuclear Deterrent Forces: Their Origins, Roles and Deployment 1946–1969: a Documentary History* (HMSO, 1994)

Royal Air Force Reserve and Auxiliary Forces (Royal Air Force Historical Society, 2003)

Royal Air Force: The Official Annual Review 2017 (Key Publishing, 2016)

WEBSITES

Royal Air Force: www.raf.mod.uk

RAF Museum: www.rafmuseum.org.uk

Oxford Dictionary of National Biography: www.oxforddnb.com

Imperial War Museums: www.iwm.org.uk

Air of Authority – A History of RAF Organisation: www.rafweb.org

Flightglobal Archive: www.flightglobal.com/pdfarchive/index.html

ACKNOWLEDGEMENTS

Thanks go to Claire Plimmer and Claire Berrisford at Summersdale, and Julian Beecroft and Emily Kearns for, as always, making the experience a pleasant and professional one. Thanks also to Des Brennan for his insights into the RAF's operations procedures; to Charles Ross, Chairman of the Lightning Association, for the definitive word on the Binbrook Boots; and to Kevin Howes, Tony Cunnane and Daniel Ferguson for sharing their experiences in uniform. Special thanks to Sir Roger Austin, for his memories and the very ideas that shaped the book itself.

R. A. Ferguson deserves a special mention for his contributions and assistance over many years, for not just this book but many others.

Have you enjoyed this book? If so, why not write a review
on your favourite website?

If you're interested in finding out more about our books,
find us on Facebook at **Summersdale Publishers** and
follow us on Twitter at **@Summersdale**.

Thanks very much for buying this Summersdale book.

www.summersdale.com